Web Application Development with R Using Shiny

Second Edition

Integrate the power of R with the simplicity of Shiny to deliver cutting-edge analytics over the Web

Chris Beeley

PACKT PUBLISHING

BIRMINGHAM - MUMBAI

Web Application Development with R Using Shiny
Second Edition

First published: October 2013

Second edition: January 2016

Production reference: 1220116

Published by Packt Publishing Ltd.
Livery Place
35 Livery Street
Birmingham B3 2PB, UK.

ISBN 978-1-78217-434-9

www.packtpub.com

Credits

Author
Chris Beeley

Reviewer
Bogdan Rau

Commissioning Editor
Nadeem Bagban

Acquisition Editors
Shaon Basu
Divya Poojari

Content Development Editor
Susmita Sabat

Technical Editor
Dhiraj Chandanshive

Copy Editors
Dipti Mankame
Rashmi Sawant

Project Coordinator
Judie Jose

Proofreader
Safis Editing

Indexer
Tejal Daruwale Soni

Production Coordinator
Shantanu N. Zagade

Cover Work
Shantanu N. Zagade

About the Author

Chris Beeley works for Nottinghamshire Healthcare NHS Trust as the lead analyst and programmer for staff and patient experience. He uses a variety of open source tools (PHP/MySQL, Apache, R, Shiny, and Ubuntu) to collect, collate, analyze, and report on patient and staff experience throughout the organization. He was the author of the previous edition of this book.

He has been a keen user of R and a passionate advocate of open source tools in research and healthcare settings, having completed his PhD. He has made extensive use of R (and Shiny) to automate analysis and report on a new patient feedback website. This was funded by a grant from the NHS Institute for Innovation and made in collaboration with staff, service users, and carers within the Trust, particularly individuals from the Involvement Centre.

I'd like to thank all the staff, service users, and carers at the Involvement Centre in Nottinghamshire Healthcare NHS Trust for welcoming me and for their ideas and support to build the best patient experience portal in the whole NHS. I believe that it's only by giving our service users a voice that we can provide high-quality care that treats people with dignity and respect. The trials and tribulations of managing the towering stack of technology, which brings the final product to the world, is made much easier because the relationship that I have with the people at the center makes the process meaningful and fun.

I'd also like to thank everyone in the R world, especially everyone at RStudio. R was my introduction to the world of open source software. Along with patient experiences, R and open source software are my great loves in life. Open source software is on the rise everywhere, including healthcare, because it's cheaper, better, and because the message of open source—that we can achieve more when we cooperate than when we compete—is a profound and urgent one.

This book is dedicated to my children, without whom all of this would be possible.

About the Reviewer

Bogdan Rau is a data science and public health practitioner, and a principal at Dataleap, a data science company. He works for data-enabled start-up companies to take the guesswork out of decision making and has implemented R and Shiny in a variety of production environments. More information can be found at `http://dataleap.io`.

www.PacktPub.com

Support files, eBooks, discount offers, and more

For support files and downloads related to your book, please visit www.PacktPub.com.

Did you know that Packt offers eBook versions of every book published, with PDF and ePub files available? You can upgrade to the eBook version at www.PacktPub.com and as a print book customer, you are entitled to a discount on the eBook copy. Get in touch with us at service@packtpub.com for more details.

At www.PacktPub.com, you can also read a collection of free technical articles, sign up for a range of free newsletters and receive exclusive discounts and offers on Packt books and eBooks.

https://www2.packtpub.com/books/subscription/packtlib

Do you need instant solutions to your IT questions? PacktLib is Packt's online digital book library. Here, you can search, access, and read Packt's entire library of books.

Why subscribe?

- Fully searchable across every book published by Packt
- Copy and paste, print, and bookmark content
- On demand and accessible via a web browser

Free access for Packt account holders

If you have an account with Packt at www.PacktPub.com, you can use this to access PacktLib today and view 9 entirely free books. Simply use your login credentials for immediate access.

Table of Contents

Preface

Harness the graphical and statistical power of R, and rapidly develop interactive and engaging user interfaces using the superb Shiny package, which makes programming for user interaction simple. R is a highly flexible and powerful tool used for analyzing and visualizing data. Shiny is the perfect companion to R, making it quick and simple to share analysis and graphics from R that users can interact with and query over the Web. Let Shiny do the hard work and spend your time generating content and styling, not writing code to handle user inputs. This book is full of practical examples and shows you how to write cutting-edge interactive content for the Web, right from a minimal example all the way to fully styled and extensible applications.

This book includes an introduction to Shiny and R and takes you all the way to advanced functions in Shiny as well as using Shiny in conjunction with HTML, CSS, and JavaScript to produce attractive and highly interactive applications quickly and easily. It also includes a detailed look at other packages available for R, which can be used in conjunction with Shiny to produce dashboards, maps, advanced D3 graphics, among many things.

What this book covers

Chapter 1, *Getting Started with R and Shiny!*, runs through the basics of statistical graphics, data input, and analysis with R. We also discuss data structures and programming basics in R in order to give you a thorough grounding in R before we look at Shiny.

Chapter 2, *Building Your First Application*, helps you build your first Shiny application. We begin with simply adding interactive content to a document written in markdown, and then delve deeper into Shiny, building a very primitive minimal example, and finally, looking at more complex applications and the inputs and outputs necessary to build them.

Chapter 3, Building Your Own Web Pages with Shiny, covers how Shiny works with existing web content in HTML, CSS, and JavaScript. We discuss the Shiny helper functions that allow you to add a custom HTML to a standard Shiny application and how to build a minimal example of a Shiny application in your own raw HTML with Shiny running in the background. Finally, we also discuss using JavaScript/ jQuery with Shiny with examples given to add bells and whistles to an existing application as well as providing powerful interactive tools to communicate between the web page and Shiny using JavaScript.

Chapter 4, Taking Control of Reactivity, Inputs, and Outputs, covers advanced functions in Shiny in detail, in particular, changing the UI based on user input or the state of the application, finely controlling reactivity in your application, and advanced methods used for reading user input as well as specialized graphics and data tables. We also cover debugging, which can pose challenges in Shiny applications.

Chapter 5, Advanced Applications I – Dashboards, contains detailed information of the layout in Shiny applications. We discuss simple ways to use layout functions described earlier in the book, and how to use the Bootstrap style on which Shiny is based. Finally, we also cover how a full dashboard is produced with several pages, specialized input and output widgets, and other advanced features accessible when using Shiny dashboards.

Chapter 6, Advanced Applications II – Using JavaScript Libraries in Shiny Applications, reviews some of the many JavaScript libraries, which can easily be integrated into Shiny, and how to use them in your own Shiny applications. We also cover how to draw graphics, which describe trends and predictions, heatmaps and highly interactive charts using D3, and 3D plots, along with an advice on how best to ensure that they work within Shiny.

Chapter 7, Sharing Your Creations, discusses the many different ways to share Shiny applications with your end users. There are many ways of doing this and they are described in detail, including the use of the Gist and GitHub website, locally using a simple ZIP file, hosting them yourself on your own server, or making use of RStudio's hosting services. We also cover reading and writing data using Shiny in a server (as opposed to a local) environment.

What you need for this book

This book can be used with the Windows, Mac, or Linux operating systems. It requires the installation of R as well as several user-contributed packages within R. R and its associated packages are all available for free. The RStudio IDE is recommended because it simplifies some of the tasks covered in this book but are not essential. Again, this software is available free of charge.

Who this book is for

This book is for anybody who wants to produce interactive data summaries over the Web, whether you want to share them with a few colleagues or the whole world. No previous experience with R, Shiny, HTML, or CSS is required to begin using this book, although you should possess some previous experience with programming in a different language.

Conventions

In this book, you will find a number of text styles that distinguish between different kinds of information. Here are some examples of these styles and an explanation of their meaning.

Code words in text, database table names, folder names, filenames, file extensions, pathnames, dummy URLs, user input, and Twitter handles are shown as follows: "We can see the separation of input code `sliderInput()` and output code `renderPlot()`."

A block of code is set as follows:

```
conditionalPanel(
  condition = "input.theTabs == 'trend'",
  checkboxInput("smooth", label = "Add smoother?", # add smoother
    value = FALSE)
)
```

When we wish to draw your attention to a particular part of a code block, the relevant lines or items are set in bold:

```
tabPanel("Trend", plotOutput("trend"),
  value = "trend")
```

Any command-line input or output is written as follows:

```
> runGitHub("basicGoogleAnalytics2ndEdition", "ChrisBeeley")
```

New terms and **important words** are shown in bold. Words that you see on the screen, for example, in menus or dialog boxes, appear in the text like this: "Navigate to **File | New | R Markdown | New document** and enter the code."

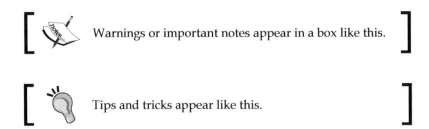

Warnings or important notes appear in a box like this.

Tips and tricks appear like this.

Reader feedback

Feedback from our readers is always welcome. Let us know what you think about this book—what you liked or disliked. Reader feedback is important for us as it helps us develop titles that you will really get the most out of.

To send us general feedback, simply e-mail feedback@packtpub.com, and mention the book's title in the subject of your message.

If there is a topic that you have expertise in and you are interested in either writing or contributing to a book, see our author guide at www.packtpub.com/authors.

Customer support

Now that you are the proud owner of a Packt book, we have a number of things to help you to get the most from your purchase.

Downloading the example code

You can download the example code files from your account at http://www.packtpub.com for all the Packt Publishing books you have purchased. If you purchased this book elsewhere, you can visit http://www.packtpub.com/support and register to have the files e-mailed directly to you.

Errata

Although we have taken every care to ensure the accuracy of our content, mistakes do happen. If you find a mistake in one of our books—maybe a mistake in the text or the code—we would be grateful if you could report this to us. By doing so, you can save other readers from frustration and help us improve subsequent versions of this book. If you find any errata, please report them by visiting http://www.packtpub.com/submit-errata, selecting your book, clicking on the **Errata Submission Form** link, and entering the details of your errata. Once your errata are verified, your submission will be accepted and the errata will be uploaded to our website or added to any list of existing errata under the Errata section of that title.

To view the previously submitted errata, go to https://www.packtpub.com/books/content/support and enter the name of the book in the search field. The required information will appear under the **Errata** section.

Piracy

Piracy of copyrighted material on the Internet is an ongoing problem across all media. At Packt, we take the protection of our copyright and licenses very seriously. If you come across any illegal copies of our works in any form on the Internet, please provide us with the location address or website name immediately so that we can pursue a remedy.

Please contact us at copyright@packtpub.com with a link to the suspected pirated material.

We appreciate your help in protecting our authors and our ability to bring you valuable content.

Questions

If you have a problem with any aspect of this book, you can contact us at questions@packtpub.com, and we will do our best to address the problem.

1
Getting Started with R and Shiny!

R is free and open source as well as being the pre-eminent tool for statisticians and data scientists. It has more than 6000 user-contributed packages, which help users with tasks as diverse as chemistry, biology, physics, finance, psychology, and medical science, as well as drawing extremely powerful and flexible statistical graphics.

In recent years, R has become more and more popular, and there are an increasing number of packages for R, which make cleaning, analyzing, and presenting data on the web easy for everybody. The Shiny package, in particular, makes it incredibly easy to deliver interactive data summaries and queries to end users through any modern web browser. You're reading this book because you want to use these powerful and flexible tools for your own content.

This book will show you how, right from starting with R, to build your own interfaces with Shiny and integrate them with your own websites. In this chapter, we're going to cover the following:

- Download and install R and choose a code editing environment/IDE
- Look at the power of R and learn about how RStudio and contributed packages can make writing code, managing projects, and working with data easier
- Install Shiny and run the examples
- Take a look at some awesome Shiny applications and some of the elements of the Shiny application we will build over the course of this book

R is a big subject, and this is a whistle-stop tour; so if you get a little lost along the way, don't worry. This chapter is really all about showing you what's out there and encouraging you to delve deeper into the bits that interest you and showing you places you can go for help if you want to learn more on a particular subject.

Installing R

R is available for Windows, Mac OS X, and Linux at `cran.r-project.org`. Source code is also available at the same address. It is also included in many Linux package management systems; Linux users are advised to check before downloading from the web. Details on installing from source or binary for Windows, Mac OS X, and Linux are all available at `cran.r-project.org/doc/manuals/R-admin.html`.

The R console

Windows and Mac OS X users can run the R application to launch the R console. Linux and Mac OS X users can also run the R console straight from the terminal by typing R.

In either case, the R console itself will look something like this:

```
R version 3.2.0 (2015-04-16) -- "Full of Ingredients"
Copyright (C) 2015 The R Foundation for Statistical Computing
Platform: x86_64-pc-linux-gnu (64-bit)

R is free software and comes with ABSOLUTELY NO WARRANTY.
You are welcome to redistribute it under certain conditions.
Type 'license()' or 'licence()' for distribution details.

  Natural language support but running in an English locale

R is a collaborative project with many contributors.
Type 'contributors()' for more information and
'citation()' on how to cite R or R packages in publications.

Type 'demo()' for some demos, 'help()' for on-line help, or
'help.start()' for an HTML browser interface to help.
Type 'q()' to quit R.

>
```

R will respond to your commands right from the terminal. Let's have a go:

```
> 2 + 2
[1] 4
```

The [1] tells you that R returned one result, in this case, 4. The following command shows how to print Hello world:

```
> print("Hello world!")
[1] "Hello world!"
```

The following command shows the multiples of pi:

```
> 1:10 * pi
[1]  3.141593  6.283185  9.424778 12.566371 15.707963 18.849556
[7] 21.991149 25.132741 28.274334 31.415927
```

This example illustrates vector-based programming in R. 1:10 generates the numbers 1:10 as a vector, and each is then multiplied by pi, which returns another vector, the elements each being pi times larger than the original. Operating on vectors is an important part of writing simple and efficient R code. As you can see, R again numbers the values it returns at the console with the seventh value being 21.99.

One of the big strengths of using R is the graphics capability, which is excellent even in a vanilla installation of R (these graphics are referred to as base graphics because they ship with R). When adding packages such as ggplot2 and some of the JavaScript-based packages, R becomes a graphical tour de force, whether producing statistical, mathematical, or topographical figures, or indeed many other types of graphical output. To get a flavor of the power of base graphics, simply type the following at the console:

```
> demo(graphics)
```

You can also type the following command:

```
> demo(persp)
```

There is more on ggplot2 and base graphics later in the chapter and a brief introduction to JavaScript and D3-based packages for R in *Chapter 6, Advanced Applications II–Using JavaScript Libraries in Shiny Applications*.

Enjoy! There are many more examples of R graphics at gallery.r-enthusiasts.com/.

Code editors and IDEs

The Windows and OSX versions of R both come with built-in code editors, which allow code to be edited, saved, and sent to the R console. It's hard to recommend that you use this because it is rather primitive. Most users would be best served by RStudio (rstudio.com/), which includes project management and version control (including support for Git, which is covered in *Chapter 7, Sharing Your Creations*), viewing of data and graphics, code completion, package management, and many other features. The following is an illustrative screenshot of an RStudio session:

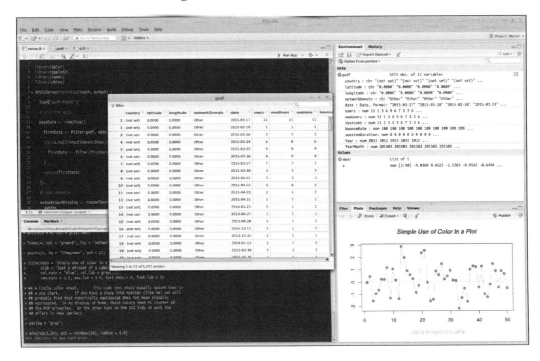

As can be seen, in the top-left corner, there is the code editing pane (with syntax highlighting). The clockwise move from there will take you to the environment pane (in which the different objects loaded into the session can be seen); the viewing pane containing various options such as **Files**, **Plots**, **Build**, **Help**, and the console (again, with syntax highlighting). In the middle, there is one of the most useful features of RStudio—the ability to view dataframes. This function also comes with sorting and filtering by column.

However, if you already use an IDE for other types of code, it is quite likely that R can be well integrated into it. Examples of IDEs with good R integration include the following:

- Emacs with the Emacs Speaks Statistics plugin
- Vim with the Vim-R plugin
- Eclipse with the StatET plugin

Learning R

There are almost as many uses for R as there are people using it. It is not possible to cover your specific needs within this book. However, it is likely that you wish to use R to process, query, and visualize data such as sales figures, satisfaction surveys, concurrent users, sporting results, or whatever types of data your organization processes. Later chapters will concentrate on Google Analytics data downloaded from the API, but for now, let's just take a look at the basics.

Getting help

There are many books and online materials that cover all aspects of R. The name R can make it difficult to come up with useful web search hits (substituting CRAN for R can sometimes help); nonetheless, searching for R tutorial brings back useful results. Some useful resources include the following:

- Excellent introduction to syntax and data structures in R (goo.gl/M0RQ5z)
- Videos on using R from Google (goo.gl/A3uRsh)
- Swirl (swirlstats.com)
- Quick-R (statmethods.net)

At the R console, `?functionname` (for example, `?help`) brings up help materials and use of `??help` will bring up a list of potentially relevant functions from installed packages.

Subscribing to and asking questions on the R-help mailing list at r-project.org/mail.html allows you to communicate with some of the leading figures in the R community as well as many other talented enthusiasts. Do read the posting guide and research your question before you ask any questions because it's a busy and sometimes unforgiving list.

There are two Stack Exchange communities, which can provide further help at `stats.stackexchange.com/` (for questions about statistics and visualization with R) and `stackoverflow.com/` (for questions about programming with R).

There are many ways to learn R and related subjects online; RStudio has a very useful list on their website available at `goo.gl/8tX7FP`.

Loading data

The simplest way of loading data into R is probably using a comma-separated value (`.csv`) spreadsheet file, which can be downloaded from many data sources and loaded and saved in all spreadsheet software (such as Excel or LibreOffice). The `read.table()` command imports data of this type by specifying the separator as a comma, or there is a function specifically for `.csv` files, `read.csv()`, as shown in the following command:

```
> analyticsData <- read.table("~/example.csv", sep = ",")
```

Otherwise, you can use the following command:

```
> analyticsData <- read.csv("~/example.csv")
```

Note that unlike in other languages, R uses `<-` for assignment as well as `=`. Assignment can be made the other way using `->`. The result of this is that y can be told to hold the value of 4 like this, `y <- 4`, or like this, `4 -> y`. There are some other more advanced things that can be done with assignment in R, but don't worry about them now. Just write code using the assignment operator in the preceding example and you'll be just like the natives that you will come across on forums and blog posts.

Either of the preceding code examples will assign the contents of the `Analytics.csv` file to a dataframe named `analyticsData`, with the first row of the spreadsheet providing the variable names. A dataframe is a special type of object in R, which is designed to be useful for the storage and analysis of data.

Data types and structures

There are many data types and structures of data within R. The following topics summarize some of the main types and structures that you will use when building Shiny applications.

Dataframes, lists, arrays, and matrices

Dataframes have several important features, which make them useful for data analysis:

- Rectangular data structures with the typical use being cases (for example, days in one month) down the rows and variables (page views, unique visitors, or referrers) along the columns.

- A mix of data types is supported. A typical dataframe might include variables containing dates, numbers (integers or floats), and text.

- With subsetting and variable extraction, R provides a lot of built-in functionality to select rows and variables within a dataframe.

- Many functions include a data argument, which makes it very simple to pass dataframes into functions and process only the variables and cases that are relevant, which makes for cleaner and simpler code.

We can inspect the first few rows of the dataframe using the `head(analyticsData)` command. The following screenshot shows the output of this command:

```
> head(analyticsData)
         Day pageViews uniqueVisitors visitDuration
1 2013-06-01       572             21      7.843611
2 2013-06-02       955             36      8.555000
3 2013-06-03       993             48     17.959722
4 2013-06-04       553             41     20.997500
5 2013-06-05       654             16     12.221111
6 2013-06-06       878             47      8.250278
>
```

As you can see, there are four variables within the dataframe—one contains dates, two contain integer variables, and one contains a numeric variable. There is more about variable types in R shown in the following paragraphs.

Variables can be extracted from dataframes very simply using the `$` operator as follows:

```
> analyticsData$pageViews
 [1] 836 676 940 689 647 899 934 718 776 570 651 816
[13] 731 604 627 946 634 990 994 599 657 642 894 983
[25] 646 540 756 989 965 821
```

Also, variables can be extracted from dataframes using `[]`, as shown in the following command:

```
> analyticsData[, "pageViews"]
```

Note the use of the comma with nothing before it to indicate that all rows are required. In general, dataframes can be accessed using `dataObject[x,y]` with x being the number(s) or name(s) of the rows required and y being the number(s) or name(s) of the columns required. For example, if the first 10 rows were required from the `pageViews` column, it could be achieved like this:

```
> analyticsData[1:10,"pageViews"]
[1]  836 676 940 689 647 899 934 718 776 570
```

Leaving the space before the comma blank returns all rows, and the space after the comma blank returns all variables. For example, the following command returns the first three rows of all variables:

```
> analyticsData[1:3,]
```

The following screenshot shows the output of this command:

```
> analyticsData[1:3,]
          Day pageViews uniqueVisitors visitDuration
1 2013-06-01       572             21      7.843611
2 2013-06-02       955             36      8.555000
3 2013-06-03       993             48     17.959722
>
```

Dataframes are a special type of list. Lists can hold many different types of data including lists. As with many data types in R, their elements can be named, which can be useful to write code that is easy to understand. Let's make a list of the options for dinner, with drink quantities expressed in milliliters.

In the following example, please note also the use of the `c()` function, which is used to produce vectors and lists by giving their elements separated by commas. R will pick an appropriate class for the return value, string for vectors that contain strings, numeric for those that only contain numbers, logical for Boolean values, and so on:

```
> dinnerList <- list("Vegetables" =
  c("Potatoes", "Cabbage", "Carrots"),
  "Dessert" = c("Ice cream", "Apple pie"),
  "Drinks" = c(250, 330, 500)
)
```

 Note that code is indented throughout, although entering directly into the console will not produce indentations; it is done for readability.

Indexing is similar to dataframes (which are, after all, just a special instance of a list). They can be indexed by number, as shown in the following command:

```
> dinnerList[1:2]
$Vegetables
[1] "Potatoes" "Cabbage"  "Carrots"


$Dessert
[1] "Ice cream" "Apple pie"
```

This returns a list. Returning an object of the appropriate class is achieved using [[]]:

```
> dinnerList[[3]]
[1] 250 330 500
```

In this case a numeric vector is returned. They can be indexed also by name:

```
> dinnerList["Drinks"]
$Drinks
[1] 250 330 500
```

Note that this, also, returns a list.

Matrices and arrays, which, unlike dataframes, only hold one type of data, also make use of square brackets for indexing, with analyticsMatrix[, 3:6] returning all rows of the third to sixth column, analyticsMatrix[1, 3] returning just the first row of the third column, and analyticsArray[1, 2,] returning the first row of the second column across all of the elements within the third dimension.

Variable types

R is a dynamically typed language and you are not required to declare the type of your variables. It is worth knowing, of course, about the different types of variable that you might read or write using R. The different types of variable can be stored in a variety of structures, such as vectors, matrices, and dataframes, although some restrictions apply as detailed previously (for example, matrices must contain only one variable type):

- Declaring a variable with at least one string in will produce a vector of strings (in R, the character data type):

  ```
  > c("First", "Third", 4, "Second")
  [1] "First"  "Third"  "4"  "Second"
  ```

You will notice that the numeral 4 is converted to a string, "4". This is as a result of coercion, in which elements of a data structure are converted to other data types in order to fit within the types allowed within the data structure. Coercion occurs automatically, as in this case, or with an explicit call to the `as()` function, for example, `as.numeric()`, or `as.Date()`.

- Declaring a variable with just numbers will produce a numeric vector:

```
> c(15, 10, 20, 11, 0.4, -4)
[1] 15.0 10.0 20.0 11.0  0.4 -4.0
```

- R includes, of course, also a logical data type:

```
> c(TRUE, FALSE, TRUE, TRUE, FALSE)
[1]  TRUE FALSE  TRUE  TRUE FALSE
```

- A data type exists for dates, often a source of problems for beginners:

```
> as.Date(c("2013/10/24", "2012/12/05", "2011/09/02"))
[1] "2013-10-24" "2012-12-05" "2011-09-02"
```

- The use of the `factor` data type tells R all of the possible values of a categorical variable, such as gender or species:

```
> factor(c("Male", "Female", "Female", "Male", "Male"),
  levels = c("Female", "Male"))
[1] Male   Female Female Male   Male
Levels: Female Male
```

Functions

As you grow in confidence with R you will wish to begin writing your own functions. This is achieved very simply and in a manner quite reminiscent of many other languages. You will no doubt wish to read more about writing functions in R in a fuller treatment, but just to give you an idea, here is a function called the `sumMultiply` function which adds together x and y and multiplies by z:

```
sumMultiply <- function(x, y, z){
  final = (x+y) * z
  return(final)
}
```

This function can now be called using `sumMultiply(2, 3, 6)`, which will return 2 plus 3 times 6, which gives 30.

Objects

There are many special object types within R which are designed to make it easier to analyze data. Functions in R can be polymorphic, that is to say they can respond to different data types in different ways in order to produce the output that the user desires. For example, the `plot()` function in R responds to a wide variety of data types and objects, including single dimension vectors (each value of y plotted sequentially) and two-dimensional matrices (producing a scatterplot), as well as specialized statistical objects such as regression models and time series data. In the latter case, plots specialized for these purposes are produced.

As with the rest of this introduction, don't worry if you haven't written functions before, or don't understand object concepts and aren't sure what this all means. You can produce great applications without understanding all these things, but as you do more and more with R you will start to want to learn more detail about how R works and how experts produce R code. This introduction is designed to give you a jumping off point to learn more about how to get the best out of R (and Shiny).

Base graphics and ggplot2

There are lots of user-contributed graphics packages in R that can produce some wonderful graphics. You may wish to take a look for yourself at the CRAN task view `cran.r-project.org/web/views/Graphics.html`. We will have a very quick look at two approaches: base graphics, so-called because it is the default graphical environment within a vanilla installation of R, and ggplot2, a highly popular user-contributed package produced by Hadley Wickham, which is a little trickier to master than base graphics, but can very rapidly produce a wide range of graphical data summaries. We will cover two graphs familiar to all, the bar chart and the line chart.

Bar chart

Useful when comparing quantities across categories, bar charts are very simple within base graphics, particularly when combined with the `table()` command. We will use the mpg dataset which comes with the ggplot2 package; it summarizes different characteristics of a range of cars. First, let's install the ggplot2 package. You can do this straight from the console:

```
> install.packages("ggplot2")
```

Alternatively, you can use the built in package functions in IDEs like RStudio or RKWard. We'll need to load the package at the beginning of each session in which we wish to use this dataset or the ggplot2 package itself. From the console type the following command:

```
> library(ggplot2)
```

We will use the `table()` command to count the number of each type of car featured in the dataset:

```
> table(mpg$class)
```

This returns a table object (another special object type within R) that contains the following columns shown in the screenshot:

```
> table(mpg$class)

   2seater    compact    midsize    minivan    pickup  subcompact        suv
         5         47         41         11        33          35         62
>
```

Producing a bar chart of this object is achieved simply like this:

```
> barplot(table(mpg$class), main = "Base graphics")
```

The `barplot` function takes a vector of frequencies. Where they are named, as here (the `table()` command returning named frequencies in table form), names are automatically included on the x axis. The defaults for this graph are rather plain; explore `?barplot` and `?par` to learn more about fine-tuning your graphics.

We've already loaded the ggplot2 package in order to use the mpg dataset, but if you have shut down R in between these two examples you will need to reload it by using the following command:

```
> library(ggplot2)
```

The same graph is produced in ggplot2 as follows:

```
> ggplot(data = mpg, aes(x = class)) + geom_bar() +
ggtitle("ggplot2")
```

This ggplot call shows the three fundamental elements of ggplot calls—the use of a dataframe (data = mpg), the setup of aesthetics (aes(x = class)), which determines how variables are mapped onto axes, colors, and other visual features, and the use of + geom_xxx(). A ggplot call sets up the data and aesthetics, but does not plot anything. Functions such as geom_bar() (there are many others, see ??geom) tell ggplot what type of graph to plot, as well as taking optional arguments, for example, geom_bar() optionally takes a position argument which defines whether the bars should be stacked, offset, or stretched to a common height to show proportions instead of frequencies.

These elements are the key to the power and flexibility that ggplot2 offers. Once the data structure is defined, ways of visualizing that data structure can be added and taken away easily, not only in terms of the type of graphic (bar, line, or scatter) but also the scales and co-ordinate system (log10; polar coordinates) and statistical transformations (smoothing data, summarizing over spatial co-ordinates). The appearance of plots can be easily changed with pre-set and user-defined themes, and multiple plots can be added in layers (that is, adding to one plot) or facets (that is, drawing multiple plots with one function call).

Line chart

Line charts are most often used to indicate change, particularly over time. This time we will use the longley dataset, featuring economic variables between 1947 and 1962:

```
> plot(x = 1947 : 1962, y = longley$GNP, type = "l",
  xlab = "Year", main = "Base graphics")
```

The x axis is given very simply by 1947 : 1962, which enumerates all the numbers between 1947 and 1962, and the type = "l" argument specifies the plotting of lines, as opposed to points or both.

The ggplot call looks a lot like the bar chart except with an x and y dimension in the aesthetics this time. The command looks as follows:

```
> ggplot(longley, aes(x = 1947 : 1962, y = GNP)) + geom_line() +
  xlab("Year") + ggtitle("ggplot2")
```

Base graphics and ggplot versions of the bar chart are shown in the following screenshot for the purposes of comparison:

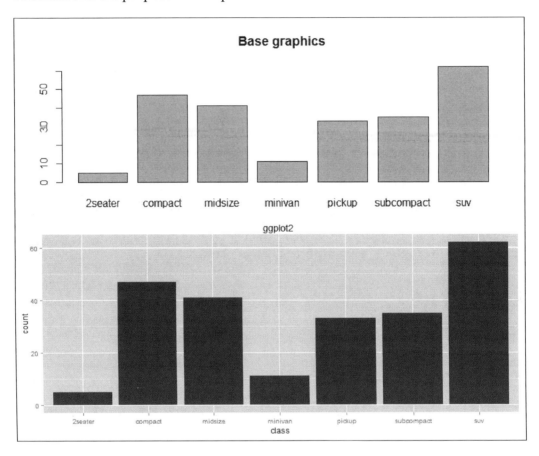

Advanced tasks with dplyr and ggvis

Just to get a taste of how easy it can be to do some really cool things with R and to start to build the foundation of the Shiny application that we are going to build through the course of this book, let's build a few graphics using some Google Analytics data and present them in an interactive document. We are going to use two contributed packages, dplyr and ggvis. The dplyr package provides very powerful functions for selecting, filtering, combining, and summarizing datasets. As you will see throughout this book, dplyr allows you to very rapidly process data to your exact specifications. The ggvis package provides very simple functions to make your visualizations interactive.

We're going to run through some of the code very quickly indeed, so you can get a feeling for some of the tasks and structures involved, but we'll return to this application later in the book where everything will be explained in detail. Just relax and enjoy the ride for now. If you want to browse or run all the code, it is available at chrisbeeley.net/website/index.html.

The Google Analytics code is not included because it requires a login for the Google Analytics API; instead, you can download the actual data from the previously mentioned link. Getting your own account for Google Analytics and downloading data from the API is covered in *Chapter 5, Advanced Applications I – Dashboards*. I am indebted to examples at goo.gl/rPFpF9 and at goo.gl/eL4Lrl for helpful examples of showing data on maps within R.

Preparing the data

In order to prepare the data for plotting, we will make use of dplyr. As with all packages that are included on the CRAN repository of packages (cran.r-project. org/web/packages/), it can be installed using the package management functions in RStudio or other GUIs, or by typing install.packages("dplyr") at the console. It's worth noting that there are even more packages available elsewhere (for example, on GitHub), which can be compiled from the source.

The first job is to prepare the data that will demonstrate some of the power of the dplyr package using the following code:

```
groupByDate =
filter(gadf, networkDomain %in% topThree$networkDomain) %>%
group_by(YearMonth, networkDomain) %>%
summarise(meanSession = mean(sessionDuration, na.rm = TRUE),
  users = sum(users),
  newUsers = sum(newUsers),
  sessions = sum(sessions))
```

This single block of code, all executed in one line, produces a dataframe suitable for plotting and uses chaining to enhance the simplicity of the code. Three separate data operations, filter(), group_by(), and summarise(), are all used, with the results from each being sent to the next instruction using the %>% operator. The three instructions carry out the following tasks:

- filter(): This is similar to subset(). This operation keeps only rows that meet certain requirements, in this case, data for which networkDomain (the originating ISP of the page view) is in the top three most common ISPs. This has already been calculated and stored within topThree$networkDomain (this step is omitted here for brevity).

- `group_by()`: This allows operations to be carried out on subsets of data points, in this case, data points subsetted by the year and month and by the originating ISP.

- `summarise()`: This carries out summary functions such as `sum` or `mean` on several data points.

So, to summarize, the preceding code filters the data to select only the ISPs with the most users overall, groups it by the year or month and the ISP, and finds the sum or mean of several of the metrics within it (`sessionDuration`, `users`, and so on).

A simple interactive line plot

We already saw how easy it is to draw line plots in ggplot2. Let's add some Shiny magic to a line plot now. This can be achieved very easily indeed in RStudio by just navigating to **File | New | R Markdown | New Shiny document** and installing the dependencies when prompted. This will create a new R Markdown document with interactive Shiny elements. R Markdown is an extension of Markdown (`daringfireball.net/projects/markdown/`), which is itself a markup language, such as HTML or LaTeX, which is designed to be easy to use and read. R Markdown allows R code chunks to be run within a Markdown document, which renders the contents dynamic. There is more information about Markdown and R Markdown in *Chapter 2*, *Building Your First Application*. This section gives a very rapid introduction to the type of results possible using Shiny-enabled R Markdown documents.

For more details on how to run interactive documents outside RStudio, refer to `goo.gl/NGubdo`. Once the document is set up, the code is as follows:

```
# add interactive UI element
inputPanel(
  checkboxInput("smooth", label = "Add smoother?", value = FALSE)
)

# draw the plot
renderPlot({
  thePlot = ggplot(groupByDate, aes(x = Date, y = meanSession,
  group = networkDomain, colour = networkDomain)) +
  geom_line() + ylim(0, max(groupByDate$meanSession))
  if(input$smooth){
    thePlot = thePlot + geom_smooth()
  }
  print(thePlot)
})
```

That's it! You'll have an interactive graphic once you run the document (click on **Run document** in RStudio or use the run() command from the rmarkdown package), as shown in the following screenshot:

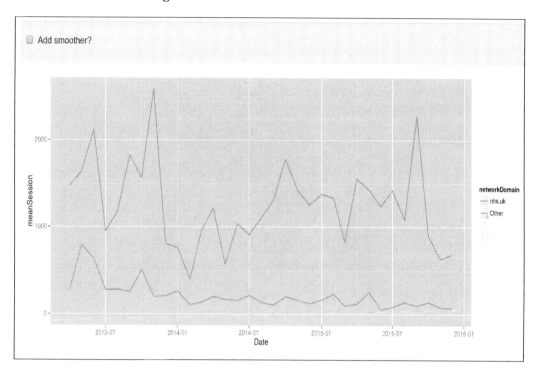

As you can see, Shiny allows us to turn on or off a smoothing line courtesy of geom_smooth() from the ggplot2 package.

Producing an interactive map (click to examine the value associated with each country) using the ggvis package is as simple as the following:

```
getUsers = function(x){
  if(is.null(x)) return(NULL)
    theCountry = head(filter(map.df, id == x$id), 1)$CNTRY_NAME
  return(filter(groupByCountry, country == theCountry)$users)
}

map.df %>%
group_by(group, id) %>%
ggvis(~long, ~lat) %>%
layer_paths(fill = ~ users) %>%
scale_numeric("fill", trans = "log", label = "log(users)") %>%
add_tooltip(getUsers, "click")  %>%
hide_axis("x") %>% hide_axis("y")
```

The final result looks like the following screenshot:

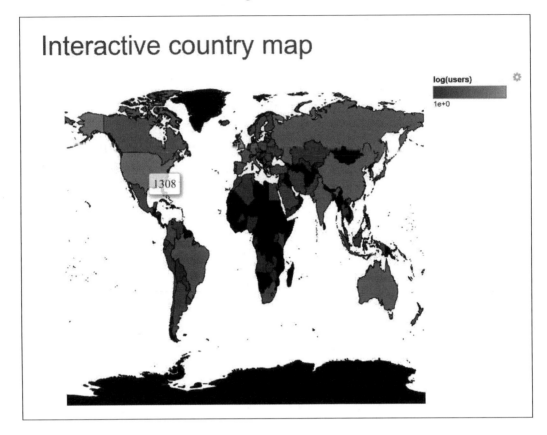

As you can see, the number of users is shown for the USA. This has been achieved simply by clicking on this country. Don't worry if you can't follow all of this code; this section is just designed to show you how quick and easy it is to produce effective and interactive visualizations.

Installing Shiny and running the examples

Shiny can be installed using standard package management functions as described previously (using the GUI or running `install.packages("shiny")` at the console).

Let's run some of the examples:

```
> library(shiny)
> runExample("01_hello")
```

Your web browser should launch and display the following screenshot (note that I clicked on the **show below** button on the app to better fit the graphic on the page):

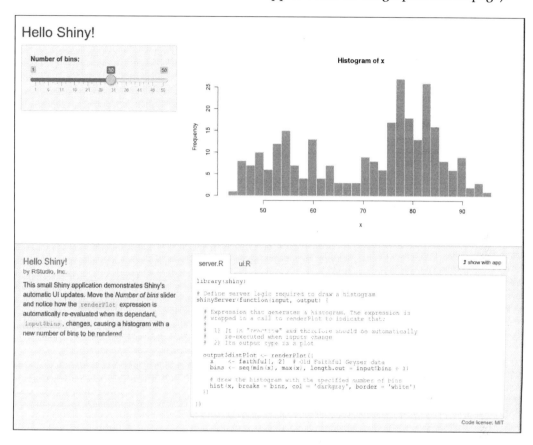

The graph shows the frequency of a set of random numbers drawn from a statistical distribution known as the normal distribution, and the slider allows users to select the size of the draw, from 0 to 1000. You will note that when you move the slider, the graph updates automatically. This is a fundamental feature of Shiny, which makes use of a reactive programming paradigm.

This is a type of programming that uses reactive expressions, which keep track of the values on which they are based that can change (known as reactive values) and update themselves whenever any of their reactive values change. So, in this example, the function that generates the random data and draws the graph is a reactive expression, and the number of random draws that it makes is a reactive value on which the expression depends. So, whenever the number of draws changes, the function re-executes.

You can find more information about this example as well as a comprehensive tutorial for Shiny at shiny.rstudio.com/tutorial/.

Also, note the layout and style of the web page. Shiny is based by default on the bootstrap theme (getbootstrap.com/). However, you are not limited by the styling at all and can build the whole UI using a mix of HTML, CSS, and Shiny code.

Let's look at an interface made with bare-bones HTML and Shiny. Note that in this and all subsequent examples, we're going to assume that you run library(shiny) at the beginning of each session. You don't have to run it before each example except at the beginning of each R session. So, if you have closed R and come back, then run it at the console. If you can't remember, run it again to be sure, as follows:

```
> runExample("08_html")
```

And here it is, in all its customizable glory:

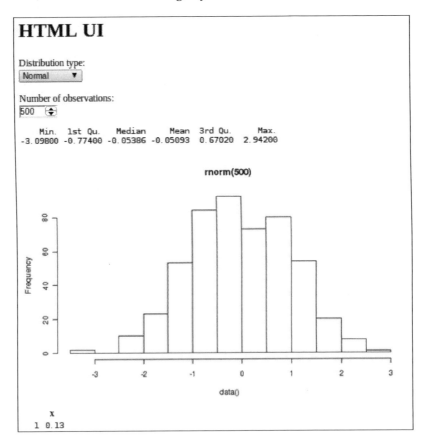

Now there are a few different statistical distributions to pick from and a different method of selecting the number of observations. By now, you should be looking at the web page and imagining all the possibilities there are to produce your own interactive data summaries and styling them just how you want, quickly and simply. By the end of the next chapter, you'll have made your own application with the default UI, and by the end of the book, you'll have complete control over the styling and be pondering where else you can go.

There are lots of other examples included with the Shiny library; just type `runExample()` at the console to be provided with a list.

To see some really powerful and well-featured Shiny applications, take a look at the showcase at `shiny.rstudio.com/gallery/`.

Summary

In this chapter, we installed R and explored the different options for GUIs and IDEs, and looked at some examples of the power of R. We saw how R makes it easy to manage and reformat data and produce beautiful plots with a few lines of code. You also learned a little about the coding conventions and data structures of R. We saw how to format a dataset and produce an interactive plot in a document quickly and easily. Finally, we installed Shiny, ran the examples included in the package, and got introduced to a couple of basic concepts within Shiny.

In the next chapter, we will go on to build our own Shiny application using the default UI.

Building Your First Application

2

In the previous chapter, we looked at R, learned some of its basic syntax, and saw some examples of the power and flexibility that R and Shiny offer. This chapter introduces the basics of Shiny. In this chapter, we're going to build our own application to interactively query results from the Google Analytics API. We will cover the following topics:

- The basic structure of a Shiny program
- The selection of simple input widgets (checkboxes and radio buttons)
- The selection of simple output types (rendering plots and returning text)
- The selection of simple layout types (page with sidebar and tabbed output panel)
- Handling reactivity in Shiny
- A brief summary of more advanced layout features

Types of Shiny application

In the first edition of this book, which was based on Shiny 0.6, there were only two types of application described. First, a fairly simple Bootstrap-themed interface with input widgets down the left and output (a single page or a tabbed output window) on the right. The second type is custom-built web pages with their own HTML and CSS files. Shiny has developed quite a bit since then, and there are actually many types of Shiny application and ways of building them. They are as follows:

- Interactive markdown documents with Shiny widgets embedded
- Shiny applications (default CSS, written entirely in R)
- Web pages (for example, custom CSS, HTML, JavaScript, and jQuery)

In this chapter, we will be considering the first two: interactive documents first and then full applications. *Chapter 3, Building Your Own Web Pages with Shiny*, will cover the building of your own web pages with Shiny applications on them.

Interactive Shiny documents in RMarkdown

Interactive documents can be made, as we saw in the previous chapter, very easily using RMarkdown in RStudio. Even if you are not using RStudio, it is a simple matter of writing an RMarkdown file with Shiny code in it. If you do not use RStudio, you will need an up to date version of Pandoc (the version in many Linux distributions is not recent enough). For more on installing Pandoc on Linux, Windows, or Mac, go to `pandoc.org/installing.html`.

RMarkdown is based on Markdown, which is a markup language designed to be easily converted into HTML but looks much more like a natural document in its raw format, as opposed to HTML or other markup languages (such as LaTeX), which have more prominent and strange-looking tags. For example, markdown syntax for a bulleted list is as follows:

```
* First bullet
* Second bullet
* Third bullet
```

The HTML equivalent is as follows:

```
<ul>
  <li>First bullet</li>
  <li>Second bullet</li>
  <li>Third bullet</li>
</ul>
```

Tagging markup in LaTeX is even more verbose. RMarkdown uses markdown conventions, but allows code chunks of R to be run within the document and text and graphical output to be generated from those chunks. Coupled with Pandoc (the Swiss Army knife of document rendering), markdown and RMarkdown can be rendered into many formats, including XHTML, HTML, epub, LaTeX, `.pdf`, `.doc`, `.docx`, and `.odt`.

RMarkdown with Shiny goes one step further and allows users to interact with the document on a web page.

Let's build a minimal example. If you are using RStudio, you will be given a boilerplate Shiny markdown document to work from, which makes things a bit easier, but here we'll ignore that and build it from scratch. The code is available at goo.gl/N7Qkv8.

Let's go through each part of the document. Navigate to **File | New | R Markdown | New document** and enter the following code:

```
# Example RMarkdown document
This is an interactive document written in *markdown*. As you can
see it is easy to include:
1. Ordered lists
2. *Italics*
3. **Bold type**
4. Links to [Documentation](http://example.com/)
## This is heading two
Perhaps this introduces the visualisation below.
```

This is the document part of the Shiny document, written in markdown. The following conventions can be noted:

- The # character is used for headings at level 1, and ## for headings at level 2
- Numbered (ordered) lists are designated with 1, 2, and so on.
- Italics are given with *single asterisks* and bold with **double asterisks**
- Links are represented like (http://example.com/)

Next follows a code chunk, beginning with ```{r} and ending with ```. The argument echo=FALSE is added to the chunk to prevent printing of the R code. You will usually want to do this, but not on every occasion, for example, when producing a teaching resource:

```
```{r, echo=FALSE}
sliderInput("sampleSize", label = "Size of sample",
  min = 10, max = 100, value = 50, step = 1)
renderPlot({
  hist(runif(input$sampleSize))
})
```
```

Straight away, we can see some of the design principles in Shiny applications. We can see the separation of input code, `sliderInput()`, and output code, `renderPlot()`. The `sliderInput()` function, as the name suggests, defines an input widget that allows the user to select from a range of numeric values, in this case, between 10 and 100, with a starting value of 50 and a step increase of 1. The `renderPlot()` function produces a reactive plot using whatever functions it finds within itself (in this case, the graphical function `hist()`, which draws a histogram).

As we already covered in *Chapter 1, Getting Started with R and Shiny!*, reactive outputs change when their inputs change. The `runif(n)` function produces *n* random numbers between 0 and 1 (with default arguments). As we can see in this case, *n* is given by `input$sampleSize`. Inputs are accessed very simply in Shiny in this format; you can see that we named the input `sampleSize` within the `sliderInput()` function, which places the selected value from the widget in `input$sampleSize` (naming it `myInput` places the value in `input$myInput`).

Therefore, `runif()` generates random numbers in the quantity of `input$sampleSize`, `hist()` plots them with a histogram, and `renderPlot({})` tells Shiny that the output within is reactive and should be updated whenever its inputs (in this case, just `input$sampleSize`) change.

The final result will look like the following screenshot:

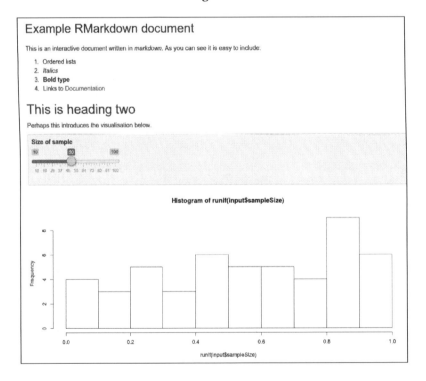

That's it! You made your first Shiny application. It's that easy. Now, let's consider building fully fledged applications, starting with a minimal example and building up from there.

A minimal example of a fully Shiny application

The first thing to note is that Shiny programs are the easiest to build and understand using two scripts, which are kept within the same folder. They should be named server.R and ui.R. Throughout this book, all code will have the commented server.R and ui.R headers to indicate which code goes in which file. The code is available at github.com/ChrisBeeley/basicGoogleAnalytics2ndEdition.

ui.R of minimal example

The ui.R file is a description of the UI and is often the shortest and simplest part of a Shiny application. Note the use of the # character, which marks lines of code as comments that will not be run, but which are for the benefit of humans producing the following code:

```
library(shiny)                            # Line 1
shinyUI(fluidPage(                        # Line 2
  titlePanel("Minimal application"),      # Line 3
  sidebarLayout(                          # Line 4
    sidebarPanel(                         # Line 5
      textInput(inputId = "comment",      # Line 6
                label = "Say something?", # Line 7
                value = "")               # Line 8
                )),                       # Line 9
    mainPanel(                            # Line 10
      h3("This is you saying it"),        # Line 11
      textOutput("textDisplay")           # Line 12
    )
  )
))
```

The following is the explanation of each line:

- Line 1: Load Shiny at the top of both files
- Line 2: Flexible layout function
- Line 3: Title
- Line 4: Standard inputs on the sidebar; outputs in the main area layout
- Line 5: The sidebar layout function
- Line 6: Give the name of the input element; this will be passed to `server.R`
- Line 7: The display label for the variable
- Line 8: The initial value
- Line 10: The output panel
- Line 11: The title drawn with the HTML helper function
- Line 12: The output text with the ID, `textDisplay`, as defined in `server.R`

To run a Shiny program on your local machine, you just need to do the following:

1. Make sure that `server.R` and `ui.R` are in the same folder.
2. Make this R's working directory (using the `setwd()` command, for example, `setwd("~/shinyFiles/minimalExample")`).
3. Load the Shiny package with the command `library(shiny)`.
4. Type `runApp()` at the console.

`runApp()` with the name of a directory within works just as well, for example, `runApp("~/shinyFiles/minimalExample")`. So instead of setting the working directory to the location of your application and then using `runApp()` separately, the whole thing can simply be carried out in one instruction, passing `runApp()` in the name of the directory directly. Just remember that it is a directory and not a file that you need to point to.

Let's have a detailed look at the file. We open it by loading the Shiny package. You should always do that in both `server.R` and `ui.R` files. The first instruction, `shinyUI(fluidPage(...` tells Shiny that we are using a fluid page layout. This is a very flexible layout function whose functionality we will explore further in *Chapter 5, Advanced Applications I – Dashboards*. The title of the application is defined next very simply using the `titlePanel()` function. There follows the main layout instruction; in this case, we are going to use the simplest UI layout, `sidebarLayout()`, which places inputs on the left (or right, optionally) and the main output section in the middle. All of the UI elements are defined within the `sidebarLayout()` function.

The next two instructions perform the main UI setup, with `sidebarPanel()` setting up the application controls and `mainPanel()` setting up the output area. `sidebarPanel()` will usually contain all of the input widgets; in this case, there is only one: `textInput()`. `textInput()` is a simple widget that collects text from a textbox that users can interact with using the keyboard. The arguments are pretty typical among most of the widgets and are as follows:

- `inputId`: This argument names the variable, so it can be referred to in the `server.R` file

- `label`: This argument gives a label to attach to the input, so users know what it does

- `value`: This argument gives the initial value to the widget when it is set up; all the widgets have sensible defaults for this argument, in this case, it is a blank string, `""`

When you start out, it can be a good idea to spell out the default arguments in your code until you get used to which function contains which arguments. It also makes your code more readable and reminds you what the return value of the function is (for example, `value = TRUE` would suggest a Boolean return).

The final function is `mainPanel()`, which sets up the output window. You can see that I used one of the HTML helper functions to make a little title `h3("...")`. There are many of these helper functions included, and they are incredibly useful for situations where you either don't want to do too much styling with HTML and CSS yourself or don't know how. Let's just stop very quickly to look at a few examples.

A note on HTML helper functions

There are several of these functions designed to generate HTML to go straight on the page; type `?p` at the console for the complete list. These functions allow you to mark up text in HTML using R code, for example, `h3("Heading 3")` producing `<h3>Heading 3</h3>`, `p("Paragraph")` producing `<p>Paragraph</p>`, and so on.

The HTML tags available through using this function include `<br>`, `<code>`, `<div>`, `<em>`, `<h1>`, `<img>`, `<p>`, `<pre>`, and `<span>`. Even more tags are available through the use of the `tags()` function. There is more on Shiny and HTML in *Chapter 3*, *Building Your Own Web Pages with Shiny*, and a full list of tags and other help is available in the documentation at `shiny.rstudio.com/articles/html-tags.html`.

The finished interface

The other element that goes in `mainPanel()` is an area to handle reactive text generated within the `server.R` file—that is, a call to `textOutput()` with the name of the output as defined in `server.R`, in this case, `textDisplay`.

The finished interface looks similar to the following screenshot:

If you're getting a little bit lost, don't worry. Basically, Shiny is just setting up a framework of named input and output elements; the input elements are defined in `ui.R` and processed by `server.R`, which then sends them back to `ui.R` that knows where they all go and what types of output they are.

server.R of minimal example

Let's look now at `server.R` where it should all become clear:

```
#####################################
##### minimal example - server.R #####
#####################################

library(shiny) # load shiny at beginning at both scripts

shinyServer(function(input, output) { # server is defined within
                                       # these parentheses

  output$textDisplay <- renderText({ # mark function as reactive
                                     # and assign to
                                     # output$textDisplay for
                                     # passing to ui.R

    paste0("You said '", input$comment,        # from the text
      "'.There are ", nchar(input$comment),    # input control as
      " characters in this."                   # defined in ui.R
    )
  })
})
```

Let's go through line by line again. We can see again that the package is loaded first using `library(shiny)`. Note that any data read instructions or data processing that just needs to be done once will also go in this first section (we'll see more about this as we go through the book). `shinyServer(...{...})` defines the bit of Shiny that's going to handle all the data. On the whole, two types of things go in here. Reactive objects (for example, data) are defined, which are then passed around as needed (for example, to different output instructions), and outputs are defined, such as graphs. This simple example contains only the latter. We'll see an example of the first type in the next example.

An output element is defined next with `output$textDsiplay <- renderText({..})`. This instruction does two basic things: First, it gives the output a name (`textDisplay`), so it can be referenced in `ui.R` (you can see it in the last part of `ui.R`). Second, it tells Shiny that the content contained within is reactive (that is, to be updated when its inputs change) and it takes the form of text. We cover advanced concepts in reactive programming with Shiny in a later chapter. There are many excellent illustrations of reactive programming at the Shiny tutorial pages available at `rstudio.github.io/shiny/tutorial/#reactivity-overview`.

The actual processing is very simple in this example. Inputs are read from `ui.R` by the use of `input$...`, so the element named in `ui.R` as `comment` (go and have a look at `ui.R` now to find it) is referenced with `input$comment`.

The whole command uses `paste0()` to link strings with no spaces (equivalent to `paste(..., sep = "")`), picks up the text the user inputted with `input$comment`, and prints it along with the number of characters within it (`nchar()`) and some explanatory text.

That's it! Your first Shiny application is ready. Using these very simple building blocks, you can actually make some really useful and engaging applications.

The program structure

Since the previous edition of this book, a significant change has taken place with regards to how Shiny applications are structured. The new feature is the ability to place them all within one code file. This is most useful when building small demonstrations or examples for other users who can just paste the whole code file at the console and have the application run automatically. In order to make use of this functionality, just combine the code from `server.R` and `ui.R` as in the following example:

```
library(shiny)
server <- function(input, output) {
  #contents of server.R file
```

```
}

ui <- fluidPage( # or other layout function
   # contents of ui.R file
)
shinyApp(ui = ui, server = server)
```

It is particularly useful neither for large applications, nor for the purposes of explaining the functions of particular parts of code within this book, so we shall ignore it from now on. Just be aware that it's possible; you may well come across it on forums, and you may wish to contribute some small examples yourself.

An optional exercise

If you want to have a practice before we move on, take the existing code and modify it so that the output is a plot of a user-defined number of observations, with the text as the title of the plot. The plot call should look like the following:

```
hist(rnorm(XXXX), main = "YYYY")
```

In the preceding line of code, XXXX is a number taken from a function in ui.R that you will add (sliderInput() or numericInput()) and YYYY is the text output we already used in the minimal example. You will also need to make use of renderPlot(); type ?renderPlot in the console for more details.

So far in this chapter, we have looked at a minimal example and learned about the basic commands that go in the server.R and ui.R files. Thinking about what we've done in terms of reactivity, the ui.R file defines a reactive value, input$comment. The server.R file defines a reactive expression, renderText(). It depends on input$comment.

Note that this dependence is defined automatically by Shiny. `renderText()` uses an output from `input$comment`, so Shiny automatically connects them. Whenever `input$comment` changes, `renderText()` will automatically run with the new value. The optional exercise gave two reactive values to the `renderPlot()` call, and so, whenever either changes, `renderPlot()` will be rerun. In the rest of this chapter, we will look at an application that uses some slightly more advanced reactivity concepts, and by the end of the book, we will have covered all the possibilities that Shiny offers and when to use them.

Embedding applications in documents

To briefly return to the subject of interactive documents, it is worth noting that it is possible to embed entire Shiny applications within interactive documents rather than having the rather stripped-down functionality that we embedded within a document earlier in the chapter. Just include a link to the directory that holds the application like this:

```{r, echo=FALSE}
shinyAppDir(
  "~/myApps/thisApplication",
  )
```

For more information about embedding, type `?shinyApp` at the console.

Widget types

Before we move on to a more advanced application, let's have a look at the main widgets that you will make use of within Shiny. I've built a Shiny application that will show you what they all look like, as well as showing their outputs and the type of data they return. To run it, just enter the following command:

```
> runGist(6571951)
```

This is one of the several built-in functions of Shiny that allow you to run code hosted on the Internet. Details about sharing your own creations in other ways are discussed in *Chapter 7, Sharing Your Creations*. The finished application looks like the following:

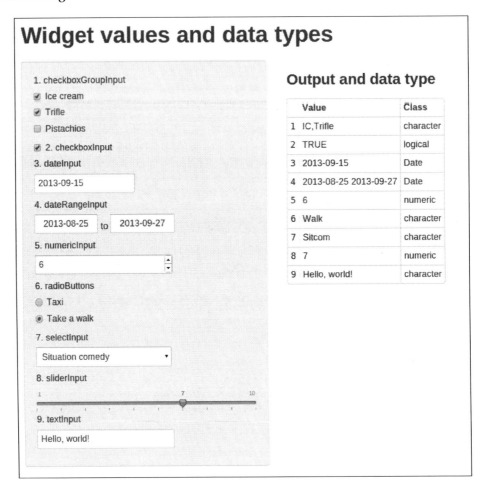

You can see the function names (checkboxGroupInput and checkboxInput) as numbered entries on the left-hand side of the panel; for more details, just type ?checkboxGroupInput at the console.

If you're curious about the code, it's available at gist.github.com/ ChrisBeeley/6571951.

The Google Analytics application

Now that we've got the basics, let's build something useful. We're going to build an application that allows you to interactively query data from the Google Analytics API. There is no room within this book to discuss registering for and using the Google Analytics API; however, you will very likely wish to make use of the wonderful RGoogleAnalytics package if you want to get your own Analytics data into R. This package is on CRAN and can therefore be installed as usual by running install.packages("RGoogleAnalytics").

To keep things simple, we will concentrate on data from a website that I worked on. We'll also use a saved copy of the data that is loaded into the application the first time it runs. A full production of the application could obviously query the API every time it is launched or on a daily or weekly basis, depending on how many users you expect (the API limits the number of daily queries from each application).

Note that we would not query the API as part of a reactive expression unless there was a clear need for the application to be constantly up to date because it would use a lot of the allocated queries, as well as making the program run a lot more slowly. In practice, this means the query, just like the data load function in this book, would be given outside of a reactive context. It is probably best to keep functions like this at the top of the shinyServer({function(input, output)...}) call just for the purposes of clarity. It will be launched each time the application is run (or it is trivially simple to write code that ensures that this only occurs once per day and the results are stored until the application is launched on the next day).

If you like any of the analysis that we come up with or want to extend it, you can always import your own Analytics data and load it in, as here, or query the API online if you want the application to be simple for others to use. All the data and code are hosted on GitHub and can be downloaded from github.com/ChrisBeeley/basicGoogleAnalytics2ndEdition.

The UI

If you can, download and run the code and data (the data goes in the same folder as the code), so you can get an idea of what everything does. If you want to run the program without copying the actual data and code to your computer (copying data and code is preferable, so you can play with it), just use another function to share and run applications (we will discuss this in *Chapter 5, Advanced Applications I – Dashboards*):

```
> runGitHub("basicGoogleAnalytics2ndEdition", "ChrisBeeley")
```

Note that setup of the `rgdal` package is necessary to run this command. This can be complex on a Linux system; see the CRAN page at `cran.r-project.org/web/packages/rgdal/index.html` for more details. In simple terms, the program allows you to select a date and time range and then view a text summary, or a plot of monthly or hourly figures. There are three tabbed windows in the output region where users can select the type of output they want (**Summary**, **Trend**, and **Map**).

The data is from a health service (known locally as the NHS) website, so users might be interested to show data that originates from domains within the NHS and compare it with data that originates from all other domains. There is an option to add a smoothed line to the graph, and three types of summary are available: a textual summary of the number of days and visitors summarized in the application, a plot of several different variables over time, and a choropleth map showing the number of visitors from different parts of the world. The following screenshot shows it in action:

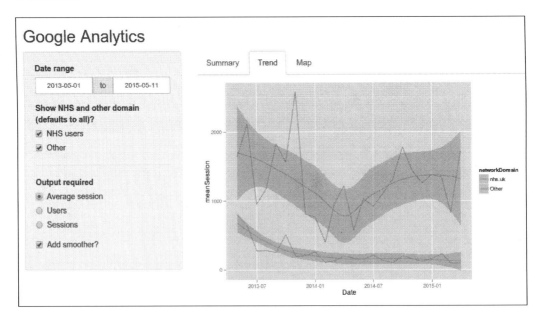

As in many Shiny applications, `ui.R` is by far the simpler of the two code files, and is as follows:

```
##############################
### Google Analytics - ui.R ###
##############################
library(shiny)
shinyUI(fluidPage( # flexible UI setup
  # Application title
  titlePanel("Google Analytics"),
  sidebarLayout( # simple setup, controls on left, output on right
    sidebarPanel( # sidebar layout
      dateRangeInput(inputId = "dateRange", label = "Date range",
        start = "2013-05-01"), # select date
```

`dateRangeInput()` gives you two nice date widgets for the user to select a start and end point. As you can see, it's given a name and a label as usual; you can specify the start and end dates (here, we've omitted the end date, which defaults to today's date, often a suitable default). There are a lot of other ways to customize, such as the way the date is displayed in the browser, whether the view defaults to months, years, or decades, and others. Type `?dateRangeInput` in the console for more information. The following code shows the `checkboxGroupInput` function:

```
checkboxGroupInput(inputId = "domainShow", # select network domain
  label = "Show NHS and other domain
  (defaults to all)?",
  choices = list("NHS users" = "nhs.uk", "Other" = "Other"),
  selected = c("nhs.uk", "Other")
),
hr(),
```

The `checkboxGroupInput()` command allows the user to select from a number of tick boxes; in this case, whether they wish to see data from users accessing the site from an NHS (the main users of the site) domain and from users from other domains. As you can see, the input is given a name and label as usual, and the checkbox inputs are specified using a named list, with the names being displayed to the user and the values being sent to the `server.R` portion of the application. Next is given `hr()`, which as you may have guessed generates the HTML `<hr/>` tag, which gives a little horizontal line, useful for visually breaking up the inputs within your interface. The following code shows the `radioButtons()` function:

```
radioButtons(inputId = "outputRequired",
  label = "Output required",
```

```
        choices = list("Average session" = "meanSession",
            "Users" = "users",
            "Sessions" = "sessions")),
```

radioButtons(), amazingly, will give you radio buttons. This allows the selection of one thing and only one thing from a list. Again, because a named list is used, an optional (...selected = ...) argument can be used to determine the default selection; otherwise, the first value is used as the default. The following code shows the checkboxInput function:

```
checkboxInput("smooth", label = "Add smoother?", # add smoother
    value = FALSE)
```

checkboxInput() very simply gives you a tickbox that returns TRUE when ticked and FALSE when unticked. This example includes all the possible arguments, which gives it a name and label and selects the initial value.

This concludes the inputs. Next, the output panel is laid out:

```
    ), # end of sidebarPanel
    mainPanel( # main panel section
        tabsetPanel( # set up tabbed output
            tabPanel("Summary", textOutput("textDisplay")
        ),
            tabPanel("Trend", plotOutput("trend")),
            tabPanel("Map", plotOutput("ggplotMap")
        )
    )
)
```

Probably the most unfamiliar part of this code is the use of tabsetPanel(). This allows multiple frames of output to be shown on the screen and selected by the user, as is common in GUIs that support tabbed frames. Note that processing is only carried out for the currently selected tab; invisible tabs are not updated behind the scenes but rather when they are made active. This is useful to know where some or all tabs require significant data processing. The setup is very simple, with a call to tabsetPanel() containing several calls to tabPanel() in which each of the tabs is defined with a heading and a piece of output as defined in server.R.

Data processing

As you write more and more complex programs, it's the `server.R` file that will become the largest because this is where all the data processing and output goes on and even where some of the functions that handle advanced UI features live. Instead of going through all of the code line by line, as we did before, we're going to look at the chunks in order and talk about the kinds of things that are done in each section in typical Shiny applications.

The first chunk of code looks like the following:

```
#####################################
#### Google Analytics - server.R #####
#####################################
library(dplyr)
library(ggplot2)
library(rgdal)
library(RColorBrewer)
library(shiny)

shinyServer(function(input, output) {
    load("gadf.Rdata")
```

The first part of this piece of code loads all of the relevant packages. Do note that in order to compile the `rgdal` package on Linux, there are dependencies on GDAL and PROJ.4. See the documentation for more details. Windows and Mac OS binaries come with these dependencies included. The `load()` function will be carried out each time the application is launched. This is where all the data preparation will take place. In this example, it is very simple and the whole dataframe is loaded in ready for use.

Sometimes, you will be able to do all of your data processing offline and load the data in being fully prepared in this way. Sometimes, however, you may rely on a spreadsheet that changes on the server regularly, or, as in this case, you may wish to query the Google API. In cases like these, this is the place to do the data cleaning and preparation necessary to run the R code with the dataset.

As noted previously, unless there is a clear reason to do so, data preparation functions would not be carried out within a reactive context because they will increase the load on the application and any data repositories it depends on (for example, the Google Analytics API). The code to do that is outside the scope of this section, but it suffices to say that as you get more confident with R, you will be analyzing more and more complex datasets and you will find it useful to do more data preparation within this section.

Reactive objects

The next section defines a reactive object. Up until now, this section has just contained a list of output commands that produce the output ready to fill the allocated spaces in `ui.R`. In the next chunk, we're going to look at another way of managing your analysis. Sometimes, you want to prepare a reactive dataset once and then pass it around the program as needed.

This might be because you have tabbed output windows (as in this case) that use the same dataset, and you don't want to write and maintain code that prepares the data according to the values of reactive inputs within all three functions. There are other times when you want to control the processing of data because it is time-intensive or it might make an online query (such as in the case of a live Google Analytics application that queries data live in response to reactive inputs).

The way that you can take more control over data processing from reactive inputs, rather than distributing it through your output code, is to use reactive objects. A reactive object, like a reactive function, changes when its input changes. Unlike a reactive function, it doesn't do anything, but is just a data object (dataframe, number, list, and so on) that can be accessed by other functions. Let's have a look at an example:

```
# reactive data
passData <- reactive({
```

Some of the R code will be a little unfamiliar to you, but for now, just concentrate on what the program is actually doing. The first thing to note is that, unlike previous examples, we are not making a call such as `output$lineGraph <- renderPlot({...})` or `output$summaryText <- renderText({...})`. Instead, we are marking whatever is inside the call as *reactive* by enclosing it in `reactive({...})`. This generates a reactive object named `passData`. This can be accessed just like any other dataframe, such as `passData()` (for the whole dataframe) or `passData()$variableName` (for a variable) or `passData()[, 2:10]` (for the second to the tenth variable). Note the brackets after `passData`:

```
firstData <- filter(gadf, date >= input$dateRange[1] &
  date <= input$dateRange[2])
```

This command filters the data by the dates that the user is interested in using the filter command from `dplyr`, using the two values from `input$dateRange` as defined in `ui.R`. Note that the first of these dates is selected with `input$dateRange[1]` and the second with `input$dateRange[2]`. This keeps your code simpler because you know that only valid values will be returned (selection of the same date is possible, so your code will need to handle that case):

```
if(!is.null(input$domainShow)){
  firstData <- filter(firstData, networkDomain %in%
    input$domainShow)
}
```

The next command further filters the data using the network domains specified within `input$domainShow`, again using the `filter` command from `dplyr`. Note the check to see if the input is `null` first; when a group of checkboxes has no return values, NULL is returned. Therefore, we can only filter when at least one is selected. The `if(!is.null()){...}` instruction ensures that we only filter when there are selections within the group checkbox.

Finally, the data is returned and the function closes as follows:

```
  return(firstData)
})
```

Outputs

Finally, the outputs are defined. Let's look first at the code that produces the first tab of output, which is the textual summary of the data.

Text summary

You will be familiar with the `paste()` command by now; the first function within the `paste()` call produces a vector of dates between the two specified in the UI and then finds its length using, unsurprisingly, the `length()` command. This is pasted together with the sum of users in the specified date range / network domains and output as a string, as shown in the following code:

```
output$textDisplay <- renderText({
  paste(
    length(seq.Date(input$dateRange[1], input$dateRange[2], by =
      "days")),
```

```
    " days are summarised. There were", sum(passData()$users),
    "users in this time period."
  )
})
```

Trend graphs

The next part of the code specifies the graph of trend in the specified variable using ggplot2. Let's look at each piece of code:

```
output$trend <- renderPlot({
  groupByDate = group_by(passData(), YearMonth, networkDomain) %>%
  summarise(meanSession = mean(sessionDuration, na.rm = TRUE),
    users = sum(users),
    newUsers = sum(newUsers), sessions = sum(sessions)
  )
```

The first line defines the output as a reactive plot, as we saw earlier in the chapter. The second instruction uses chained dplyr instructions, as we saw in *Chapter 1, Getting Started with R and Shiny!*, first, to group the data according to the YearMonth variable (which gives each date as numeric values of year and month, 201501, 201502, 201503, and so on) and the network domain variable (to select NHS and non-NHS originating requests).

Second, the summarise() function summarizes several values of the grouped dataset, taking the mean session duration and the sum of users and new users, as can be seen in the code. Put together, these instructions produce summarized session durations, users, and new users across the month/year and network domain groupings, which we desire. Let's have a look at the first 10 rows of the dataframe, which the instruction returns, to better understand what dplyr returns:

```
> groupByDate
Source: local data frame [50 x 6]
Groups: YearMonth

   YearMonth networkDomain meanSession users newUsers sessions
1     201304         Other    280.2000     6        3        7
2     201304        nhs.uk   1473.2222    13        8       15
3     201305         Other    791.9000    24        5       43
4     201305        nhs.uk   1641.0214    33        7       54
5     201306         Other    635.8060    77       41      104
6     201306        nhs.uk   2116.0000    98       56      132
7     201307         Other    277.1419   174      121      198
8     201307        nhs.uk    950.9048   284      202      332
9     201308         Other    283.0294   124       87      145
10    201308        nhs.uk   1181.4535   213      130      258
..       ...           ...         ...   ...      ...      ...
```

As you can see, there are values calculated for each combination of the two grouping variables: `YearMonth` and `networkDomain`. This allows us to easily select what we want in the plot, as we will see shortly:

```
groupByDate$Date <- as.Date(paste0(groupByDate$YearMonth, "01"),
  format = "%Y%m%d")
```

This line produces a date from the `YearMonth` variable by appending `01` to the end of the variable (in order to pick the first of the month each time), which gives 20130401, 20130501, and so on, and converts to the R Date format, which specifies the format since this is a non-standard format for conversion from string to date. For more on specifying non-standard date formats in R, type `?strptime` at the console. The ggplot package plots handle dates very nicely, so the data is now ready to be plotted:

```
thePlot <- ggplot(groupByDate,
  aes_string(x = "Date",
    y = input$outputRequired,
    group = "networkDomain",
    colour = "networkDomain"
  )
) +
geom_line()
```

This is the main setup of the plot. Note that by assigning it to `thePlot`, we do not print it, but merely begin to build it up. Note the use of `aes_string()` instead of the more usual `aes()`. This allows us to pass the string from `input$outputRequired` straight into ggplot. The standard `aes()` only accepts variable names and will not take strings in this way:

```
if(input$smooth){
  thePlot <- thePlot + geom_smooth()
}
print(thePlot)
})
```

The next section tests for the value of the smoothing checkbox, `input$smooth`, and if it is TRUE, a smoothing line is added to the plot. The requirement to `print()` ggplot graphics has been dropped from Shiny (in the previous version of this book, it was necessary to `print()` each graphic). This graphic will need to be printed in any environment, even the console, because it has not been called with `ggplot()`, but merely assigned to `thePlot`. Normally, when using `ggplot()` directly in a Shiny session, there will be no need to `print()` the plot.

A map of users across the world

The final tab produces a choropleth map, which is a map shaded according to the values of a variable. The code within this section that produces the map is based on the answer present at stackoverflow.com/questions/22625119/choropleth-world-map. As described in the answer, it relies on a shapefile hosted at geocommons.com/overlays/33578.zip:

```
output$ggplotMap <- renderPlot ({
  groupCountry <- group_by (passData (), country)
  groupByCountry <- summarise (qroupCountry, meanSession =
    mean (sessionDuration),
    users = log (sum (users)),
    sessions = log (sum (sessions))
  )
```

The first section sets up a reactive plot and uses the group_by() and summarise() commands from dplyr, which we encountered before, to summarize several of the variables by country. Note that the summed variables are also logged because almost all of the data comes from the UK and so the scale is very long. Logging the variables compresses the scale and makes it more readable:

```
world <- readOGR (dsn = ".", layer =
  "world_country_admin_boundary_shapefile_with_fips_codes")
countries <- world@data
countries <- cbind (id = rownames (countries), countries)
countries <- merge (countries, groupByCountry, by.x =
  "CNTRY_NAME",
  by.y = "country", all.x = TRUE)
map.df <- fortify (world)
map.df <- merge (map.df, countries, by = "id")
```

The next section carries out the processing with respect to the map. This is out of the scope of this discussion, but you can see that the countries data is merged with the groupByCountry data and the resulting object merged with map.df on their common column ID. This gives a link between the map and the values of interest, which can then be plotted using ggplot as follows:

```
ggplot (map.df, aes (x = long, y = lat, group = group)) +
geom_polygon (aes_string (fill = input$outputRequired)) +
geom_path (colour = "grey50") +
scale_fill_gradientn (colours = rev (brewer.pal (9, "Spectral")),
  na.value = "white") +
coord_fixed () + labs (x = "", y = "")
})
```

Again, the exact workings of the ggplot call are a little bit out of the scope of this discussion; a map is included in this chapter to demonstrate to you how easily you can produce quite advanced analytics in Shiny applications using tens of lines of code, not hundreds of lines. Do note the use of `aes_string()`, which is again used to allow `input$outputRequired` to be passed straight in to ggplot.

A note on the application code

Please note that, as at many points in this book, some of the decisions made around the `server.R` file were made to keep the code understandable and would not be used in a full application. In particular, the code that draws the map takes a long time to run, and in a full application, there are a variety of methods that could be used to reduce the load on the application, including moving some of the processing outside of a reactive call and limiting the number of times the map is updated, possibly by asking the user to press a button to refresh the map.

The latter method will be described in more detail in *Chapter 4, Taking Control of Reactivity, Inputs, and Outputs*. The code has been written not only to show a reasonably sensible setup of a Shiny application, but also to keep the code relatively simple. In the rest of the book, you will learn more about bottlenecks and possible areas where code could be made easier to maintain, which you will want to use in your own applications.

An optional exercise

The Google Analytics application is reasonably intuitive and well-featured (it doesn't, admittedly, compare all that favorably with Google's own offering!). However, as with the `server.R` code, some of the decisions around the UI setup were made for simplicity for the purposes of this book, to avoid flooding you with new widgets and ways of handling inputs in the second chapter. You may like to pause here and take a bit of time to update the code with some of the other UI elements Shiny offers to make the application function a bit more intuitively. Have a browse through the documentation yourself (`?shiny`) or make use of the following:

- `numericInput()`: This function gives both a textbox and a selection box to allow users to select a numeric value. This could be used to constrain the number of users from each country, which allows you to draw a map of just low or high use areas.
- `selectInput()`: This function allows a user to select one or multiple items from a list. This could be used to select particular countries; for example, excluding all traffic from the trend graph except from users in the UK.
- `textInput()`: This allows users to enter text. It could be used to give graphs configurable titles.

You will need to look at the return types for each of the widgets and make sure that the server.R code will accept them and, if not, change the code so that it will.

Those with some experience with R will no doubt be itching to fix the server.R file to clear up the issues outlined in the previous section. This will mainly sharpen your R skills and will also give you practice in some of the basics of scoping, classing, and passing data in a Shiny application. So, if you feel up to it, have a go with this code too.

Advanced layout features

In this chapter, we have covered the most simple of the layout features in Shiny with the help of the sidebarLayout(), mainPanel(), and tabsetPanel() functions. In later chapters, we will build larger and more complex applications, including dashboards, and make use of more advanced layout features. It is worth pausing here briefly to take a quick look at the other types of layout that are available, so you can think about the best way to implement your own application as we go through the next couple of chapters.

There are essentially two more broad types of layout function that you can use in Shiny. The first uses the layout features of Bootstrap and allows you to precisely define the layout of your application using a grid layout. Essentially, Bootstrap asks you to define the UI as a series of rows. Each row can be further subdivided into columns of varying widths.

Each set of columns on a row has widths that add up to 12. In this way one can quite easily specify, for example, the first row as consisting of one column of width 12, and then the second row as consisting of two columns, one of width 2 and one of width 10. This creates a header panel across the top of the screen and then two columns below, a thin one and a thick one, which you are likely to put UI and output elements in respectively. A whole variety of layouts is possible, and nesting and offset of columns are both possible, which means that with the right code you can build any grid-based layout you can think of. We will look in detail at the code to implement custom layouts in this way in later chapters.

The second layout feature which may prove useful to you is navbarPage(). This allows you to create several completely separate applications, with their own custom UIs and outputs, and select them from a bar which appears at the top of the screen. Custom layout features can be applied as usual within each element of the application.

Summary

In this chapter we have covered a lot of ground. We've seen that Shiny applications are generally made up of two files: `server.R` and `ui.R`. You've learned what each part of the code does, including setting up `ui.R` with the position and type of inputs and outputs and `server.R` with the data processing functions, outputs, and any reactive objects that are required.

The optional exercises have given you a chance to experiment with the code files in this chapter, varying the output types, using different widgets, and reviewing and adjusting their return values as appropriate. You've learned about the default layout in Shiny, `sidebarLayout()`, as well as about the use of `mainPanel()` and `tabsetPanel()`.

You've also learned about reactive objects and we've discussed when you might use reactive objects. There's more on finely controlling reactivity later in the book.

In the next chapter you're going to learn how to integrate Shiny with your own content, using HTML, CSS, and JavaScript.

3
Building Your Own Web Pages with Shiny

So, we built our own application to query our site's data on Google Analytics. You learned about the basic setup of a Shiny application and saw a lot of the widgets. It will be important to remember this basic structure because we are going to cover a lot of different territories in this chapter, and as a consequence, we won't have a single application at the end, as we did in the previous chapter, but lots of bits and pieces that you can use to start building your own content from.

Building one application with all of these different concepts would create several pages of code, and it would be difficult to understand which part does what. As you go through the chapter, you might want to rebuild the Google Analytics application or another of your own if you have one, using each of the concepts. If you do this, you will have a beautifully styled and interactive application by the end that you really understand. Otherwise, you might like to just browse through and pick out the things that you are particularly interested in; you should be able to understand each section on its own. Let's get started now.

We are going to cover the following areas:

- Customizing Shiny applications, or whole web pages, using HTML
- Styling your Shiny application using CSS
- Turbocharging your Shiny application with JavaScript and jQuery
- Incorporating shiny content within another web page

Running the applications and code

For convenience, I have gathered together all the applications in this chapter. The link to the live versions as well as source code and data on my website can be found at chrisbeeley.net/website. If you can, run the live version first and then browse the code as you go through each example.

Shiny and HTML

It might seem quite intimidating to customize the HTML in a Shiny application, and you may feel that by going under the hood, it would be easy to break the application or ruin the styling. You may not want to bother rewriting every widget and output in HTML just to make one minor change to the interface.

In fact, Shiny is very accommodating, and you will find that it will quite happily accept a mix of Shiny code and HTML code produced by you using Shiny helper functions and the raw HTML written by you. So, you can style just one button or completely build the interface from scratch and integrate it with some other content. I'll show you all of these methods and give some hints about the type of things you might like to do with them. Let's start simple by including some custom HTML in an otherwise vanilla Shiny application.

Custom HTML links in Shiny

This application makes use of data downloaded from a website I use a lot in my daily work, Patient Opinion (patientopinion.org.uk/). Patient Opinion lets users of health services tell their stories, and my organization makes extensive use of it to gather feedback about our services and improve them. This application uses data downloaded from the site and allows users to see the rate at which stories are posted that relate to different parts of the organization. A custom HTML button will take them straight from the application and onto the search page on Patient Opinion for that service area.

ui.R

Let's take a look at the ui.R file first:

```
####################################
### custom HTML output - ui.R ###
####################################
```

```
library(shiny)
shinyUI(fluidPage(
  tags$head(HTML("<link
    href='http://fonts.googleapis.com/css?family=Jura'
    rel='stylesheet' type='text/css'>")),

  h2("Custom HTML", style = "font-family: 'Jura'; color: green;
    font-size: 64px;"),

  sidebarLayout(
    sidebarPanel(
      radioButtons("area", "Service area",
        c("Armadillo", "Baboon", "Camel", "Deer", "Elephant"),
        selected = "Armadillo")
    ),

    mainPanel(
      h3("Total posts"),
      HTML("<p>Cumulative <em>totals</em> over time</p>"),
      plotOutput("plotDisplay"),
      htmlOutput("outputLink")
    )
  )
))
```

There's a quick method of styling text inline in this example. First, let's fetch a font from Google Fonts, which you can see in a simple matter of using the `tags$` function to generate an HTML `<head>` and then placing the link inside:

```
tags$head(HTML("<link
  href='http://fonts.googleapis.com/css?family=Jura'
  rel='stylesheet' type='text/css'>"))
```

Now we have the font available; it's a simple matter of placing it within the application. The `titlePage()` argument, which is often used at the top of a Shiny application, has been removed and replaced with `h2()` because `h2()` will allow you to insert inline styling straight into the function, whereas `titlePage()` will not. Moreover, although the accepted arguments are different, the actual HTML generated by `titlePage()` and `h2()` are the same. To test this yourself, go to the console and type `titlePage("Test")` and then try `h2("Test")`.

In both cases, the same thing is returned – `<h2>Test</h2>`. This is a really useful way of learning more about Shiny and helping you to debug more complex applications, which make use of Shiny functions as well as HTML and CSS. Sometimes, it can be necessary to run the application and then inspect the HTML using the inspect source function available in most web browsers (Chrome, Explorer, Firefox, Safari, and so on). Running the function directly at the console is a lot quicker and less confusing. Having done this, it's a simple matter of passing styling information into `h2()`, as you would pass inline styling into a font in HTML:

```
style = "font-family: 'Jura'; color: green; font-size: 64px;"
```

Also included is the `HTML()` function, which marks text strings as HTML, avoiding the HTML escaping, which would otherwise render this on the screen verbatim. The other new part of this file is the `htmlOutput()` function. This, as the `HTML()` function, prevents HTML escaping and allows you to use your own markup, but this time for text passed from `server.R`. Here's the final interface:

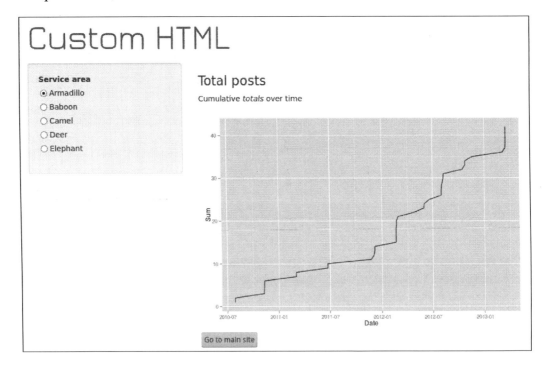

server.R

There are only a couple of new commands from Shiny in this example, so let's sharpen our R skills while we are here. The `server.R` file in this example, unlike many of the others throughout the book, deliberately does a lot of data management and cleans up at the top, before the reactive code. In this case, of course, I could have cleaned the data first and then loaded the clean data in the example.

However, very often, you will not have this luxury either because results are loaded online from an API or because your users will drop their own spreadsheets into the application folder, or some other reason like this. So, let's look at a more realistic example and put aside Shiny commands for the moment.

server.R – data preparation

Let's look at the data preparation code first:

```
##########################################
##### custom HTML output - server.R ###
##########################################

library(shiny)
library(ggplot2)

# load the data- keeping strings as strings
PO <- read.csv("PO.csv", stringsAsFactors = FALSE)

# create a new variable to hold the area in and fill with blanks
PO$Area <- NA

# find posts that match service codes and label them
# with the correct names
PO$Area[grep("RHARY", PO$HealthServices,
  ignore.case = TRUE)] <- "Armadillo"
PO$Area[grep("RHAAR", PO$HealthServices,
  ignore.case = TRUE)] <- "Baboon"
PO$Area[grep("RHANN-inpatient", PO$HealthServices,
  ignore.case = TRUE)] <- "Camel"
PO$Area[grep("rha20-25101", PO$HealthServices,
  ignore.case = TRUE)] <- "Deer"
PO$Area[grep("rha20-29202", PO$HealthServices,
  ignore.case = TRUE)] <- "Elephant"
```

```
# create a postings variable to add together for a
# cumulative sum- give it 1
PO$ToAdd <- 1

# remove all missing values for Area
# (since they will never be shown)
PO <- PO[!is.na(PO$Area),]

# API returns data in reverse chronological order- reverse it
PO <- PO[nrow(PO):1,]

# produce cumulative sum column
PO$Sum <- ave(PO$ToAdd, PO$Area, FUN = cumsum)

# produce a date column from the data column in the spreadsheet
PO$Date <- as.Date(substr(PO$dtSubmitted, 1, 10),
   format = "%Y-%m-%d")
```

After loading the Shiny package and any other necessary packages, a comma delimited spreadsheet (.csv) is loaded with the read.csv() command. Very often, you will want to use stringsAsFactors = FALSE. Factor is a special class in R, which is useful for statistical applications. A full discussion on the properties of the factor class is rather outside the scope of this book.

For now, it is sufficient to say that if you have any strings in your spreadsheet that you want to treat as strings (for example, extracting characters, coercing other variable types such as date, and so on), do ensure that you import them as strings and not as factors as done in the previous example. If you want to use factors for certain particular variables (particularly for ggplot2, which can require factors for some arguments), you can always coerce them later on. Data preparation proceeds as follows:

- A new variable is created and filled with R's missing data value, NA. The missing data value is of great use in a lot of R code; here, we are using it so that we can easily discard all the data points that fail to match to areas.

- The subset operator [] is then used with the grep() command (familiar to Unix-like OS users and which returns the positions of a character vector matching a search string). This marks all the rows of the newly created empty variable that matches each service code (a unique identifier for each different provider of health services) with a name that is meaningful to the end users.

- A helper variable ToAdd is then given a value of 1 for all the rows. This will be used to calculate the cumulative total of posts for each area.

- `PO[!is.na(PO$Area),]` is used to return all the rows of the dataset that do not have missing values for the area variable (that is, failed to match). `!is.na(x)` is a useful function that returns the positions of all the nonmissing values of x.

- The API for the website returns the data in reverse chronological order, so it is flipped over using the row indices `nrow(PO):1`, that is, a sequence of integers starting at the number of rows of the data and going down to 1.

- The `ave()` function is used to return the cumulative sum (`cumsum`) for each grouping (`PO$Area`).

- The date string (which has the time appended) is shrunk to the correct size using `substr()` and coerced to R's date class using `as.Date()`. The date class can often trip up newcomers, so it is worth having a good read of `?as.Date()`. Coercing a character string and not a factor, and ensuring that you specify the format of the string properly should get you over the common pitfalls.

Again, don't worry too much if you don't follow all of the R code. Learning R is really a book to itself. I've included it here to help you get used to the kind of things that you might want to do and to show you the commonly used shortcuts and pitfalls for beginners. Let's have a look at the `server.R` file.

server.R – the server definition

This file produces a plot of the cumulative totals of postings and produces a nicely formatted HTML button ready to post straight into the UI:

```
shinyServer(function(input, output) {
  output$plotDisplay <- renderPlot({
    # select only the area as selected in the UI
    toPlot = PO[PO$Area == input$area, ]
    ggplot(toPlot, aes(x = Date, y = Sum)) + geom_line()
  })

  output$outputLink <- renderText({
    # switch command in R as in many other programming languages
    link <- switch(input$area,
      "Armadillo" =
      "http://www.patientopinion.org.uk/services/rhary",
      "Baboon" =
      "http://www.patientopinion.org.uk/services/rhaar",
      "Camel" = "http://www.patientopinion.org.uk/services/RHANN-
      inpatient",
```

```
      "Deer" = "http://www.patientopinion.org.uk/services/rha20-
      25101",
      "Elephant" =
      "http://www.patientopinion.org.uk/services/rha20-29202"
    )
    # paste the HTML together
    paste0('<form action="', link, '"target="_blank">
      <input type="submit" value="Go to main site">
    </form>')
  })
})
```

You can see the subsetting again carried out with our old friend `[]` and a `ggplot()` call in the plot function.

The HTML button is created very easily using the `switch()` command, and `paste0()`, which concatenates strings with no spaces. With that, our newly created object `output$ouputLink` is ready to be sent straight to the UI and included as raw HTML.

A minimal HTML interface

Now that we have dipped our toes into HTML, let's build a (nearly) minimal example of an interface entirely in HTML. To use your own HTML in a Shiny application, create the `server.R` file as you normally would. Then, instead of a `ui.R` file, create a folder named www and place a file named `index.html` inside this folder. This is where you will define your interface.

index.html

Let's look at each chunk of `index.html` in turn:

```
<!---------------------------->
<!--Minimal example- HTML UI -->
<!---------------------------->

<html>
  <head>
    <title>HTML minimal example</title>
    <script src="shared/jquery.js"
    type="text/javascript"></script>
    <script src="shared/shiny.js" type="text/javascript"></script>
    <link rel="stylesheet" type="text/css"
    href="shared/shiny.css"/>
```

```
<style type = "text/css">
  body {
    background-color: #ecf1ef;
  }

  #navigation {
    position: absolute;
    width: 300px;
  }

  #centerdoc {
    max-width: 600px;
    margin-left: 350px;
    border-left: 1px solid #c6ec8c;
    padding-left: 20px;
  }
</style>
</head>
```

The `<head>` section contains some important setup for Shiny, loading the JavaScript and jQuery scripts, which make it work, as well as a style sheet for Shiny. You will need to add some CSS of your own unless you want every element of the interface and output to be displayed as a big jumble at the bottom of the screen, and the whole thing to look very ugly. For simplicity, I've added some very basic CSS in the `<head>` section; you could, of course, use a separate CSS file and add a link to it just as `shiny.css` is referenced.

The body of the HTML contains all the input and output elements that you want to use, and any other content that you want on the page. In this case, I've mixed up a Shiny interface with a picture of my cats because no web page is complete without a picture of a cat! Have a look at the following code:

```
<body>
  <h1>Minimal HTML UI</h1>
  <div id = "navigation">
    <p>
      <label>Title for graph:</label><br />
      <textarea name="comment" rows = "4"
      cols = "30">My first graph</textarea>
    </p>
    <div class="attr-col shiny-input-radiogroup" id="graph">
      <p>
```

```
          <label>What sort of graph would you like?</label><br>
          <input type="radio" name="graph" value="1"
            title="Straight line" checked>Linear<br>
          <input type="radio" name="graph" value="2"
            title="Curve">Quadratic<br>
        </p>
      </div>
      <label>Here's a picture of my cats</label><br />
      <img src="cat.jpg" alt="My cats" width="300" height = "300">
    </div>

    <div id = "centerdoc">
      <div id="textDisplay" class="shiny-text-output"></div>
      <br/>
      <div id="plotDisplay" class="shiny-plot-output"
      style="width: 80%; height: 400px"></div>
    </div>
  </body>
</html>
```

There are three main elements: a title and two `<div>` sections, one for the UI and one for the output. The UI is defined within the navigation `<div>`, which is left aligned. Recreating Shiny widgets in HTML is pretty simple, and you can also use HTML elements that are not given in Shiny. Instead of replacing the `textInput()` widget with `<input type="text">` (which is equivalent), I have instead used `<textarea>`, which allows more control over the size and shape of the input area.

The `radioButtons()` widget can be recreated with `<input type = "radio">`. You can see that both get a name attribute, which is referenced in the `server.R` file as `input$name` (in this case, `input$comment` and `input$graph`). You will note that there is another `<div>` around the radio button definition, `<div class="attr-col shiny-input-radiogroup" id="graph">`. This is a known bug within Shiny 0.12, as discussed at `goo.gl/Lrx9GB`. Another advantage of using your own HTML is that you can add tooltips; I have added these to the radio buttons using the `title` attribute.

The output region is set up with two `<div>` tags: one that is named `textDisplay` and picks up `output$textDisplay`, as defined in `server.R`, and the other that is named `plotDisplay` and picks up `output$plotDisplay` from the `server.R` file. In your own code, you will need to specify the class, as shown in the previous example, as either `shiny-text-output` (for text), `shiny-plot-output` (for plots), or `shiny-html-output` (for tables or anything else that R will output as HTML). You will need to specify the height of plots (in px, cm, and so on) and can optionally specify width either in absolute or relative (%) terms.

Just to demonstrate that you can throw anything there that you like, there's a picture of my cats underneath the UI. You will, of course, have something a bit more sophisticated in mind. Add more <div> sections, links, pictures, and whatever you like.

server.R

Let's take a quick look at the server.R file:

```
##############################################
##### minimal example for HTML- server.R #####
##############################################

library(shiny)
shinyServer(function(input, output) {
  output$textDisplay <- renderText({
    paste0("Title:'", input$comment,
      "'. There are ", nchar(input$comment),
      " characters in this."
    )
  })

  output$plotDisplay <- renderPlot({
    par(bg = "#ecf1ef") # set the background color
    plot(poly(1:100, as.numeric(input$graph)), type = "l",
      ylab="y", xlab="x")
  })
})
```

Text handling is done as before. You'll note that the renderPlot() function begins by setting the background color to the same as the page itself (par(bg = "#ecf1ef") and for more graphical options in R, see ?par). You don't have to do this, but the graph's background will be visible as a big white square if you don't.

The actual plot itself uses the poly() command to produce a set of numbers from a linear or quadratic function according to the user input (that is, input$graph). Note the use of as.numeric() to coerce the value we get from the radio button definition in index.html from a string to a number.

This is a common source of errors in Shiny code, and you must remember to keep track of how variables are stored, whether as lists, strings, or other variable types, and either coerce them in place (as done here), or coerce them all in one go using a reactive function.

The latter option can be a good idea to make your code less fiddly and buggy because it removes the need to keep track of variable types in every single function you write. There is more about defining your own reactive functions and passing data around a Shiny instance in the next chapter. The `type ="l"` argument returns a line graph, and the `xlab` and `ylab` arguments give labels to the x and y axes.

The following screenshot shows the finished article:

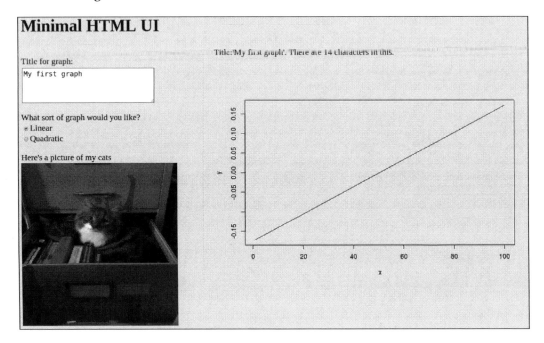

JavaScript and Shiny

With Shiny, JavaScript, and jQuery, you can build pretty much anything you can think of; moreover, Shiny and jQuery will do a lot of the heavy lifting, which means that fairly minimal amounts of code will be required. We are going to take a look at another couple of *toy* examples.

Please note that these examples do NOT represent best practice in coding. They do not make the best use of CSS, HTML, or jQuery. They are just there to demonstrate the principles and show you how easy it is. In your own applications, you will want to make use of HTML, JavaScript (and/ or jQuery), and CSS in the most appropriate and efficient way.

The connection between JavaScript and Shiny is another reason to recommend RStudio as an IDE because it performs beautiful syntax highlighting on JavaScript straight out of the box (although, clearly, other text editors and IDEs may do this or be easily configured to do so).

Before we proceed, it's worth reviewing the difference between server- and client-side code and what they're used for. JavaScript gained popularity as a client-side language, which ran on web browsers and added interactivity to websites that would otherwise be static HTML and CSS files, which were downloaded from servers.

It has found increasing use on the server side (for example, with Node.js), but we are going to use it client side and so will not consider this any further. So, in this case, JavaScript is running client side. The server side, in this case, of course, is R, and specifically the commands are to be found in the `server.R` file. Shiny and JavaScript (and, by extension, jQuery) can, as server and client, respectively, pass things back and forth between themselves as you wish.

Also, it's worth noting that there are in fact two ways to Shiny and JavaScript to interact with each other:

- The first is perhaps the simplest and will be considered first. Because Shiny and JavaScript can both read and write to the web page (that is, to the **Document Object Model (DOM)**), it is quite simple for them to interact with each other on the webpage. The DOM is a way of organizing objects in HTML, XHTML, and XML documents, in which elements are referenced within a tree structure.

> A detailed discussion is well outside the scope of this book; suffice to say that if you are going to use JavaScript with Shiny or HTML, you will need to learn about the DOM and how to get and set attributes within it.

- The second way in which Shiny and JavaScript can interact is for when it's easier or better to send messages directly between the server and client. Although in theory you could use the `<input type="hidden">` tag of HTML and pass messages on the DOM without showing them to the user, it will often be easier to cut out the middle man and send the information directly, particularly when the message is complicated (a large JSON object, for instance).

We will look at sending messages directly after the first example. Once we've covered JavaScript, we will briefly cover how to incorporate jQuery into your applications, which will allow you to produce attractive and interactive outputs with very little code.

First, as a warm-up, we will look at using JavaScript to read the DOM generated by Shiny and perform some client-side processing, before writing the changes back to the DOM.

Example 1 – reading and writing the DOM

In this example, we're going to read some user-supplied text from the DOM, grab it with JavaScript, and write an animation back to the DOM. We'll look at the `ui.R` and `server.R` file to put together the page first and finish with the JavaScript.

ui.R

This example also includes more examples related to including custom HTML without writing the whole thing out in HTML yourself. Let's take a look at the `ui.R` file:

```
################################################
#### Animating text with JavaScript- ui.R #####
################################################

library(shiny)
shinyUI(fluidPage( # flexible layout function
  titlePanel("Animating text"),
  sidebarLayout(
    sidebarPanel( # sidebar configuration
      h3("Let's animate something!"),          # heading helper
      p("Please enjoy the animation responsibly"), # paragraph helper
      tags$textarea(id = "textArea", "Go!"),    # tags$XX for
                                                #   generating HTML

      tags$input(type = "button",
        id = "animate", value = "Animate!",
        onClick = "buttonClick()")              # reference to JS
      ),
      mainPanel(
        h3("Ready... set..."),
        tags$canvas(id = "myCanvas",            # graphical
                                                #   output area
```

```
        width = "500", height = "250"),
      includeHTML("textSend.js"),                    # include JS file
      textOutput("textDisplay")
    )
  )
))
```

There are two things in this file that you haven't seen before. The first is the tags$xxx() function, which will generate HTML for you. The tags$textarea(id="textArea", "Go!") call generates the following:

```
<textarea id="textArea" class="shiny-bound-input">Go!</textarea>.
```

Similarly, the whole tags$input(...) call generates the following:

```
<input type="button" id="animate" value="Animate!"
  onclick="buttonClick()">
```

The second thing that you haven't seen before is the includeHTML() function. This allows you to link to a file that contains a lot of HTML (in this case, a JavaScript definition), rather than cluttering up your ui.R with it. You could very well include plain HTML using this function.

server.R

The server.R file is unchanged from our original minimal example:

```
######################################################
##### Animating text with JavaScript - server.R ####
######################################################

library(shiny)
shinyServer(function(input, output) {
  output$textDisplay <- renderText({
    # handle Shiny text function
    paste0("You said '", input$textArea,
      "'. There are ", nchar(input$textArea),
      " characters in this."
    )
  })
})
```

Of course, you can do much more processing than this if you wish. The JavaScript file (textSend.js) contains no surprises and functions just as it does in any other web application:

```
<script type="text/javascript">
function buttonClick(){
  // get and set up the drawing canvas
  var c = document.getElementById("myCanvas");
  var ctx = c.getContext("2d");
  ctx.font = "30px Arial";

  // get the text from the UI
  var text = document.getElementById("textArea").value;

  // set up positional variables
  var textX = 150;
  var textY = 1;

  // define move function
  function move(){
    ctx.clearRect(0, 0, c.width, c.height);
    ctx.fillText(text, textX, textY * 5);
    if(textY++ < 40){
      setTimeout(move, 25); // delay between frames
    }
  }
  move(); // call function
}
</script>
```

We won't look in detail at the JavaScript because that is rather out of the scope of this discussion. There are two code chunks – the first, which picks up the drawing canvas we drew in the ui.R file using document.getElementById("myCanvas"). This is a very useful function if you can find the name of the element on the DOM, either by running the code directly from ui.R in the R console or examining the HTML source on your browser, as we discussed before, then you can grab it with JavaScript using this function.

The next couple of lines set it up ready for drawing. The second code chunk picks up the input from the textarea that we defined in ui.R. The rest of the code just draws the text on the screen and then animates it so that it falls down the frame. Here is a screenshot of the application:

You will, I am sure, wish to produce something a little more sophisticated than this! Now we have the basics, the second example is a bit more complex. In this example we will be passing messages directly between server (R) and client (JavaScript).

Example 2 – sending messages between client and server

In this example, we are going to use the DOM and messages to pass information in between the client and server. The user will be able to select a number using a slider. The server reads this input and then picks a random number between 1 and the user-supplied number. This number is written back to the screen as well as being sent in a message to JavaScript.

JavaScript receives this number and produces a drop-down selector that allows the user to select a value between 1 and the random number that the server picked. Every time the user selects a different value on this dropdown, JavaScript will decide randomly whether it thinks that "Shiny rules!" or whether, in fact, "JavaScript rules!". This is sent as a message to the server, which picks it up and writes it to the screen. Clearly, this is not of much use as a real application, but it should demonstrate to you the principles of sending and receiving messages and reading and writing to the DOM.

It is definitely worth having a look at the application live, as with all the applications it can be run straight from my website chrisbeeley.net/website, where the source code can also be downloaded. Here is the application in action:

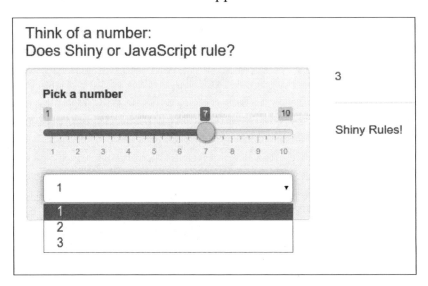

As you can see, the user has picked **7**, the server has picked **3** out of the range of numbers 1 to 7, JavaScript has built a drop-down menu using that number of options and has also decided in this case that Shiny rules. Do note that this application could quite easily be written in pure Shiny using the methods described in the next chapter, and like many examples in this book, is provided for illustration only. We will look at more advanced uses of JavaScript later in the book, but for now, it is worth keeping it simple, so you can see easily how everything fits together without worrying about understanding everything the JavaScript is doing.

In this case, the ui.R and server.R files are both pretty simple and should be fairly self-explanatory. Most of the code is in the JavaScript file. Let's quickly look at the ui.R and server.R files first.

ui.R

The code runs as follows:

```
#################################################
#### Running JavaScript on the page - ui.R ####
#################################################

library(shiny) # load Shiny at the top of both files
shinyUI(fluidPage(
```

```
# flexible layout function
h4(HTML("Think of a number:</br>Does Shiny or </br>JavaScript
  rule?")),
sidebarLayout(
  sidebarPanel(
    # sidebar configuration
    sliderInput("pickNumber", "Pick a number",
    min = 1, max = 10, value = 5),
    tags$div(id = "output") # tags$XX for holding dropdown
  ),

  mainPanel(
    includeHTML("dropdownDepend.js"), # include JS file
    textOutput("randomNumber"),
    hr(),
    textOutput("theMessage")
  )
)
))
```

The use of h4(HTML("XXX")) allows us to shrink the title a little and add some
HTML line breaks (avoiding HTML escaping with the HTML function as before).
The tags$div(...) produces a <div> element in which to place the drop-down
menu, which JavaScript will build. The mainPanel() call just contains a reference to
the JavaScript file that will run on the page, a place to put the random number the
server will pick, a horizontal line, and a message from JavaScript regarding whether
JavaScript or Shiny rules.

server.R

The server.R file runs as follows:

```
####################################################
#### Running JavaScript on the page - server.R ####
####################################################

library(shiny)
shinyServer(function(input, output, session) {
  output$randomNumber = renderText({
    theNumber = sample(1:input$pickNumber, 1)
    session$sendCustomMessage(type = 'sendMessage',
      message = theNumber)
    return(theNumber)
  })
```

```
    output$theMessage = renderText({
      return(input$JsMessage)
    })
  })
})
```

The first thing to note here is the use of `shinyServer(function(input, output, session){...})` instead of `shinyServer(function(input, output){...})` that we are used to seeing. The addition of a session argument adds a considerable amount of functionality to Shiny applications. In this case, it allows us to send messages to JavaScript. There is more on the functionality of the session argument in the next chapter.

The first function here carries out two tasks. First, it takes the number that the user selected on the slider and picks a random number between 1 and that number. It sends that number straight to JavaScript using the `session$sendCustomMessage` function (which the session argument mentioned previously enables). The `sendCustomMessage()` function is defined within Shiny; it is placed after `session$` in order to tie it to the session defined in the `shinyServer(function(input, output, session){...})` function. Finally, it returns the number to Shiny, just like in a standard application, ready to be placed in the output slot, which `ui.R` sets up.

The second function receives the JavaScript message. It's very easy to access, the Shiny function within JavaScript writes it to the standard `input$xxx` variable name, which we are used to seeing throughout the book. As is now plain, a lot of the work in this application is being done within the JavaScript file. Let's take a look.

dropdownDepend.js

There is quite a lot of code in this section doing quite a lot of different things, so we'll step through each chunk in turn:

```
<script type="text/javascript">
  // Shiny function to receive messages
  Shiny.addCustomMessageHandler("sendMessage",
    function(message) {
      // call this before modifying the DOM
      Shiny.unbindAll();
```

The first part carries out two functions, `Shiny.addCustomMessageHandler("sendMessage", function(message){...})` registers the message handler with Shiny. The name `"sendMessage"` was defined in the `server.R` function in the `session$sendCustomMessage(type = 'sendMessage', message = theNumber)` call. This is the first step in receiving and processing messages from the server.

The second part begins the process of reading and writing to the DOM. Whenever you are going to modify the DOM in JavaScript, you should call `Shiny.unbindAll()` first and then `Shiny.bindAll()` at the end; we will come across the latter function later in this section.

```
/* delete the dropdown if it already
exists which it will the second
time this function is called */

// get the dropdown and assign to element
var element = document.getElementById('mySelect');

// if it already exists delete it
if (element !== null) {
  element.parentNode.removeChild(element);
}
```

In this section, we check to see if the dropdown has already been drawn, which of course it will be the second time this function is called, and if it has, we delete it in order to redraw it with the new number of options.

```
// Create empty array to store the options
var theNumbers = [];

// add ascending numbers up to the
// value of the message
for (var i = 1; i <= message; i++) {
  theNumbers.push(i);
}

// grab the div ready to write to it
var theDiv = document.getElementById("output");
```

Now we create an array and fill it with the numbers from 1 to the value of message, which is the random number that the server picked and passed to this function.

```
// create a new dropdown
var selectList = document.createElement("select");

// give it a name and write it to the div
selectList.setAttribute("id", "mySelect");
theDiv.appendChild(selectList);
```

```
      // add the options
      for (var n = 0; n < theNumbers.length; n++) {
        var option = document.createElement("option");
        option.setAttribute("value", theNumbers[n]);
        option.text = theNumbers[n];
        selectList.appendChild(option);
      }
```

Next, we create the drop-down list and add the options to it using the array of numbers created immediately before.

```
      // add an onchange function to call shinyRules
      // every time this input changes
      selectList.onchange = shinyRules;

      // add class to style nicely in Bootstrap
      selectList.className += "form-control";

      // call this when you've finished modifying the DOM
      Shiny.bindAll();
    }
  );
```

Finally, we add on onchange property to the dropdown so that it will call the shinyRules() function every time it is changed, add the class form-control to render the dropdown nicely in Bootstrap, and call the Shiny.bindAll() function necessary when we have finished writing the DOM, which was described previously.

```
    shinyRules = function(){
      // define text array and pick random element
      var textArray = ['JavaScript Rules!', 'Shiny Rules!'];
      var randomNumber = Math.floor(Math.random()*textArray.length);

      // whenever this input changes send a message to the server
      Shiny.onInputChange("JsMessage", textArray[randomNumber]);
    }
  </script>
```

This last piece of code defines the function shinyRules(), which, as in the preceding code, will be called each time the dropdown is changed. It sets up a text array, picks a random element from it, and then uses the Shiny.onInputChange (...) function to send this element to the server. As you can see, the function takes two arguments in this case: "JsMessage" and textArray[randomNumber].

The first of these arguments gives the message a name, so it can be picked up by the `server.R` file. This is the part of the `server.R` file that we saw before that reads `input$JsMessage`, so the input is accessed using the standard Shiny notation of `input$xxx` that we are used to seeing. If you go back to look at the `server.R` file, you can see a call to `renderText()` that returns `input$JsMessage`, ready to be written straight to the output panel of the interface.

Take a step back and rewind

We covered quite a lot of material in this section, so it's worth spending a moment reviewing what we covered. There are two main ways to use JavaScript in your applications. The first one is probably the simplest for most purposes; it involves using the capabilities of Shiny and JavaScript to read and write to the DOM. If you want the intermediate steps to be visible on the screen and want to carry out extra processing (either in Shiny or JavaScript), then reading and writing to the DOM directly provides a simple-to-code method of doing this.

When you want to hide intermediate steps, for example, passing something from Shiny to JavaScript, processing it at client side, and sending it back again without showing any of the intermediate steps, or when you have complex messages to send between client and server (for example, JSON objects), it can be easier to take control yourself and pass them back and forth manually without using the DOM. In reality, either approach can be used in any situation (since elements you write to the DOM can be made invisible) and the real decision will come down to how simple, transparent, and easy to maintain you can make your code using each approach.

Inputs and outputs built with JavaScript can be registered with Shiny and become an integral part of the application just like the components generated within Shiny, as opposed to being abstracted from it (either via the DOM or custom messages). This is a bit more complex.

jQuery

For the ultimate quick and clean code, let's add some jQuery. We are going to add mouseover row highlighting (that is, coloring in rows of a table when the mouse pointer is on them) for a table from Shiny. As we noted at the beginning of this section, this chapter merely gives you ideas and shows you how to carry out certain functions. Using jQuery for mouseover row highlighting is not the best practice because it can be very easily performed using CSS. Also, in the following code, we will allow the user to bold individual cells by clicking on them as well as producing a pop-up information box about the dataset.

index.html – the body

We'll skip the head for now and look at the body of the `index.html` file:

```
<body>
  <h1>jQuery example</h1>
  <div id = "navigation">
    <label for="dataSet">Select dataset</label>
    <select id="dataSet">
      <option value="iris" selected="selected">
        Iris data
      </option>
      <option value="USPersonalExpenditure">
        Personal expenditure data
      </option>
      <option value="CO2">
        CO2 data
      </option>
    </select>
  </div>

  <div id = "centerdoc">
    <div id="datatext" class="shiny-text-output"></div>
    <div id="hiddentext" style = "text-indent: 100%;
        white-space: nowrap; overflow: hidden"
        class="shiny-text-output">
    </div>
    <div id="dataset" class="shiny-html-output"></div>
  </div>
</body>
```

The interface, as you can see, allows users to select one of three datasets, which are included in R. There are two outputs that are visible: some text and a table that will be specified within the `server.R` file (you can see them previously, the `<div>` sections with `id = "datatext"` and `id = "dataset"`). A further `<div>` section (with `id = "hiddentext"`) allows R to generate some text, so make it available to jQuery but without displaying it on the screen until the user requests it. Let's now look at the `server.R` file.

server.R

Following is the `server.R` file:

```
library(shiny)
shinyServer(function(input, output) {
  output$dataset <- renderTable({
```

```
theData = switch(input$dataSet,
  "iris" = iris,
  "USPersonalExpenditure" = USPersonalExpenditure,
  "CO2" = CO2)
head(theData)
})

output$datatext <- renderText({
  paste0("This is the ", input$dataSet, " dataset")
})

output$hiddentext <- renderText({
  paste0("Dataset has ", nrow(switch(input$dataSet,
    "iris" = iris,
    "USPersonalExpenditure" = USPersonalExpenditure,
    "CO2" = CO2)),
  "rows")
})
})
```

The function within `renderTable()` quite simply takes the string sent from the interface and returns the dataset within R with the same name. It then displays the first few rows of the dataset using `head()`, which is returned as an HTML table. There are two calls made to `renderText()`, as can be seen. The first returns a text string describing which dataset has been selected. The second returns a description of how many rows there are in the dataset. This will be hidden from the user and is only accessible via jQuery.

Before we go into detail, here is the finished interface:

jQuery example

Select dataset Iris data   This is the iris dataset

	Sepal.Length	Sepal.Width	Petal.Length	Petal.Width	Species
1	5.10	3.50	1.40	0.20	setosa
2	4.90	3.00	1.40	0.20	setosa
3	**4.70**	3.20	1.30	0.20	setosa
4	4.60	3.10	1.50	0.20	setosa
5	5.00	3.60	1.40	0.20	setosa
6	5.40	3.90	1.70	0.40	setosa

As you can see in the previous screenshot, the first row is highlighted. This is achieved through a mouseover (which works on any row). The third value of Sepal. Length is in bold, and this is achieved through a mouse click. Double-clicking on the text above the table brings up a message about the dataset, as shown in the following screenshot:

This, of course, is the text that we generated and hid, as we saw in the server.R and index.html files. Let's look at the jQuery to do this.

This, of course, is the text that we generated and hid, as we saw in the server.R and index.html files. Let's look at the jQuery to do this as mentioned previously, you can keep the jQuery code wherever you like: in a text file, verbatim in the <head> of your HTML or using a call to includeHTML() from an ui.R file. As usual, wrap your code in the following manner:

```
$(document).ready(function(){
   ...
})
```

Please note that mouseover code will normally look like the following:

```
$('tr').mouseover(function(){
   $(this).css('background-color', 'yellow');
});
```

However, in this case, it will not work. This is because your output will be redrawn, and so you will need to access all the elements that will be drawn as well as those that already are. Rewrite the previous code in the following manner (it is a piece of code from Joe Cheng of RStudio):

```
$(document).on("mouseover", "tr", function(evt) {
   $(this).css('background-color', 'yellow');
})
```

The previous is the `mouseover` code that handles row highlighting, and following is the `mouseout` code to put it back to normal once the pointer leaves:

```
$(document).on("mouseout", "tr", function(evt) {
  $(this).css('background-color', 'transparent');
});
```

Applying bold effects to individual cells is achieved through the following code snippet. As you can see, the function starts by clearing bold formatting from all the cells (in case a different cell has already been highlighted by the user) and then bolds the cell that has been clicked:

```
$(document).on("click", "td", function(evt) {
  $('td').css('font-weight', 'normal');
  $(this).css('font-weight', 'bold');
})
```

Finally, the following code snippet describes a function that listens for a double-click on the text that describes the dataset and then gives more information about the data, which we have placed on the screen and hidden:

```
$(document).on("dblclick", "#datatext", function(evt) {
  alert($('#hiddentext').text());
})
```

As with the JavaScript example, none of these functions are going to win any prizes for UI design, but they do hopefully illustrate some general things that are very easy to accomplish. Following are some examples of things you might like to try in your own applications:

- Click to expand sets of rows in large tables
- Custom highlighting of table cells within a user-set range (note that this can be done without jQuery, using pure Shiny code, but it is more difficult like this).
- Mouseover helps text to provide additional documentation for a Shiny application

Exercise

If you haven't already been tempted, now is definitely a good time to have a go at building your own application with your own data. The next chapter covers advanced topics in Shiny and, though you are welcome to plough on, a little practical experience with the functions will stand you in good stead for the next chapter. If you're interested in sharing your creations right away, feel free to jump to *Chapter 7, Sharing Your Creations*.

How you go about building your first application will very much depend on your previous experience and what you want to achieve with Shiny, but as with everything in life, it is better to start simple. Start with the minimal example given in the previous chapter and put in some data that's relevant to you. Shiny applications can be hard to debug (compared with interactive R sessions, at least), so in your early forays, keep things very simple.

For example, instead of drawing a graph, start with a simple `renderText()` call and just print the first few values of a variable. This will at least let you know that your data is loading okay and the server and UI are communicating properly. Always make sure that any code you write in R (graphs, tables, data management, and so on) works in a plain interactive session, before you put it into a Shiny application!

Debugging

Probably the most helpful and simple debugging technique is to use `cat()` to print to the R console. There are two main reasons why you should do this:

- The first is to put in little messages to yourself, for example, `cat("This branch of code executed")`

- The second is to print the properties of R objects if you are having problems relating to data structure, size, or type. `cat(str(x))` is particularly useful and will print a little summary of any kind of R object, whether it is a list, a dataframe, a numeric vector, or anything else

The other useful method is a standard method of debugging in R, `browser()`, which can be put anywhere in your code. As soon as it is executed, it halts the application and enters the debug mode (see `?browser`). There is more on debugging Shiny applications in the next chapter.

Once you have the application working, you can start to add custom HTML using Shiny's built-in functions or rewrite `ui.R` into `index.html`. The choice here really depends on how much HTML you want to include. Although in theory, you can create very large HTML interfaces in Shiny using `.html` files referenced by the `includeHTML()` command, you will end up with a rather confusing list of markups scattered across different files.

Rewriting to raw HTML is likely to be the easier option in most cases. If you are already proficient in JavaScript and/or jQuery, then you may like to have a go using them with a Shiny application. If not, you can leave this for now or perhaps just modify the code included in this chapter to see if you can get different and interesting effects.

Bootstrap 3 and Shiny

Since the first edition of this book, Shiny has migrated from Bootstrap 2 to Bootstrap 3. There are now many functions, both within Shiny and in packages (such as shinyBS and shinythemes, both available on CRAN), which enhance the way you can style your applications straight from Shiny. There is more on advanced layout functions, Bootstrap 3, and packages to help you to style your applications in *Chapter 5, Advanced Applications I – Dashboards.*

Summary

This chapter has put quite a heap of tools in your Shiny toolbox. You learned how to use custom HTML straight from a minimal ui.R UI setup and how to build the whole thing from scratch using HTML and CSS. You also looked at some data management and cleaning in R and some examples of Shiny applications using JavaScript and jQuery. Hopefully, by now, you should have made your own application, whether in pure Shiny or with your own HTML markup, and perhaps experimented with JavaScript or jQuery.

In the next chapter, you are going to learn more about higher control over Shiny applications, including controlling reactivity, scoping and passing variables, and a variety of input/output functions.

4

Taking Control of Reactivity, Inputs, and Outputs

So far in this book, we've mastered the basics of Shiny by building our own Google Analytics application as well as looked at how to style and extend Shiny applications using HTML, CSS, and JavaScript. In this chapter, we are going to extend our toolkit by learning about advanced Shiny functions. These allow you to take control of the fine details of your application, including the interface, reactivity, data, and graphics.

In order to do this, we're going to go back to the Google Analytics application and totally upgrade it, making it much smoother, more intuitive, and well-featured. The finished code and data for this advanced Google Analytics application can be found at github.com/ChrisBeeley/GoogleAnalytics2ndEdition.

In this chapter, we will cover the following topics:

- Learning how to show and hide parts of the interface
- Changing the interface reactively
- Finely controlling reactivity, so functions and outputs run at the appropriate time
- Using URLs and reactive Shiny functions to populate and alter the selections within an interface
- Uploading and downloading data to and from a Shiny application
- Producing beautiful tables with the DataTables jQuery library
- Using custom graphics and animations in Shiny
- Showing progress bars to users in long running functions
- Debugging Shiny code

What's new in our application?

We're going to add a lot of new functionality to the application, and it won't be possible to explain every piece of code before we encounter it. Several of the new functions depend on at least one other function, which means that you will see some of the functions for the first time while a different function is being introduced.

It's important, therefore, that you concentrate on whichever function is being explained and wait until later in the chapter to understand the whole piece of code. New functions that are explained later in the chapter will be noted as we progress. In order to help you understand what the code does as you go along, it is worth quickly reviewing the actual functionality of the application now. You can find a link to a hosted version of the application within the GitHub page referenced in the introduction to this chapter. It is definitely worth visiting this page to see the application in action yourself.

In terms of the functionality, which has been added to the application, it is now possible to select not only the network domain from which browser hits originate but also the country of origin. The draw map function now features a button in the UI, which prevents the application from updating the map each time new data is selected, the map is redrawn only when the button is pushed. This is to prevent minor updates to the data from wasting processor time before the user has finished making their final data selection.

A **Download report** button has been added, which sends some of the output as a static file to a new web page for the user to print or download. An animated graph of trend has been added; this will be explained more fully in the relevant section and, finally, a table of data has been added, which summarizes mean values of each of the selectable data summaries across the different countries of origin.

Downloading data from RGoogleAnalytics

We did not cover using the RGoogleAnalytics API in detail in *Chapter 2, Building Your First Application*, and won't here either because it's a little outside of the scope of this book. The Google Analytics application in this book makes use of the RGoogleAnalytics package mentioned in *Chapter 2, Building Your First Application*. The code is given and briefly summarized in the following section to give you a feel for how to use it.

Note that my username and password have been replaced with xxxx. You can get your own user details from the Google Analytics website. Also note that this code is not included on the GitHub because it requires the username and password to be present in order for it to work.

```
library(RGoogleAnalytics)

### Generate the oauth_token object
oauth_token <- Auth(client.id = "xxxx",
  client.secret = "xxxx")

# Save the token object for future sessions
save(oauth_token, file = "oauth_token")
```

Once you have your `client.id` and `client.secret` from the Google Analytics website, the preceding code will direct you to a browser to authenticate the application and save the authorization within `oauth_token`. This can be loaded in future sessions to save you from reauthenticating each time.

```
# Load the token object and validate for new run
load("oauth_token")
ValidateToken(oauth_token)
```

The preceding code will load the token in subsequent sessions. The `validateToken()` function is necessary each time because the authorization will expire after a time; this function will renew the authentication.

```
## list of metrics and dimensions
query.list <- Init(start.date = "2013-01-01",
  end.date = as.character(Sys.Date()),
  dimensions = "ga:country,ga:latitude,ga:longitude,
    ga:networkDomain,ga:date",
  metrics = "ga:users,ga:newUsers,ga:sessions,
    ga:bounceRate,ga:sessionDuration",
  max.results = 10000,
  table.id = "ga:71364313")
gadf = GetReportData(QueryBuilder(query.list), token =
  oauth_token, paginate_query = FALSE)
```

Finally, the metrics and dimensions of interest (for more on metrics and dimensions, refer to the documentation of the Google Analytics API online) are placed within a list and downloaded with the `GetReportData()` function.

```
... [data tidying functions]...
save(gadf, file = "gadf.Rdata")
```

The data tidying that is carried out at the end is omitted here for brevity; as you can see at the end, the data is saved as `gadf.Rdata` ready for loading within the application.

Animation

Animation is surprisingly easy. The `sliderInput()` function, which gives an HTML widget that allows the selection of a number along a line, has an optional animation function that will increment a variable by a set amount every time a specified unit of time elapses. This allows you to very easily produce a graphic that animates.

In the following example, we are going to look at the monthly graph and plot a linear trend line through the first 20% of the data (0–20% of the data). Then, we are going to increment the percentage value that selects the portion of the data by 5% and plot a linear through that portion of data (5–25% of the data). Then, increment again 10–30% and plot another line, and so on.

There is a static image in the following screenshot:

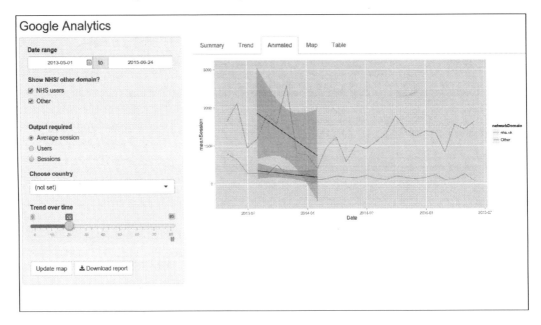

The slider input is set up as follows, with an ID, label, minimum value, maximum value, initial value, step between values, and the animation options, giving the delay in milliseconds and whether the animation should loop:

```
sliderInput("animation", "Trend over time",
  min = 0, max = 80, value = 0, step = 5,
  animate = animationOptions(interval = 1000,
    loop = TRUE))
```

Having set this up, the animated graph code is pretty simple, looking very much like the monthly graph data except with the linear smooth based on a subset of the data instead of the whole dataset. The graph is set up as before and then a subset of the data is produced on which the linear smooth can be based:

```
groupByDate <- group_by(passData(), YearMonth, networkDomain) %>%
summarise(meanSession = mean(sessionDuration, na.rm = TRUE),
  users = sum(users),
  newUsers = sum(newUsers), sessions = sum(sessions))
groupByDate$Date <- as.Date(paste0(groupByDate$YearMonth, "01"),
  format = "%Y%m%d")
smoothData <- groupByDate[groupByDate$Date %in%
  quantile(groupByDate$Date,
    input$animation / 100,
    type = 1) : quantile(groupByDate$Date,
    (input$animation + 20) / 100,
    type = 1),]
```

We won't get too distracted by this code, but essentially, it tests to see which of the whole date range falls in a range defined by percentage quantiles based on the `sliderInput()` values. Take a look at `?quantile` for more information.

Finally, the linear smooth is drawn with an extra data argument to tell ggplot2 to base the line only on the smaller `smoothData` object and not the whole range:

```
ggplot(groupByDate, aes_string(x = "Date",
  y = input$outputRequired,
  group = "networkDomain",
  colour = "networkDomain")) + geom_line() +
  geom_smooth(data = smoothData,
    method = "lm", colour = "black")
```

Not bad for a few lines of code. We have both ggplot2 and Shiny to thank for how easy this is.

Streamline the UI by hiding elements

This is a simple function that you are certainly going to need if you build even a moderately complex application. Those of you who have been doing extra credit exercises and/or experimenting with your own applications will probably have already wished for this or, indeed, have already found it.

`conditionalPanel()` allows you to show or hide UI elements based on other selections within the UI. The function takes a condition (in JavaScript, but the form and syntax will be familiar from many languages) and a UI element, and displays the UI only when the condition is `true`. This is actually used a couple of times in the advanced GA application, and indeed in all the applications, I've ever written of even moderate complexity.

We're going to show the option to smooth the trend graph only when the trend graph tab is displayed, and we're going to show the controls for the animated graph only when the animated graph tab is displayed.

Naming tabPanel elements

In order to allow testing for which tab is currently selected, we're going to have to first give the tabs of the tabbed output names. This is done as follows (with the new code in bold):

```
tabsetPanel(id = "theTabs", # give tabsetPanel a name
  tabPanel("Summary", textOutput("textDisplay"),
    value = "summary"),
  tabPanel("Trend", plotOutput("trend"),
    value = "trend"),
  tabPanel("Animated", plotOutput("animated"),
    value = "animated"),
  tabPanel("Map", plotOutput("ggplotMap"),
    value = "map"),
  tabPanel("Table",
    DT::dataTableOutput("countryTable"),
    value = "table")
```

As you can see, the whole panel is given an ID (`theTabs`) and then each `tabPanel` is also given a name (`summary`, `trend`, `animated`, `map`, and `table`). They are referred to in the `server.R` file very simply as `input$theTabs`.

Finally, we can make our changes to `ui.R` to remove parts of the UI based on tab selection:

```
conditionalPanel(
  condition = "input.theTabs == 'trend'",
  checkboxInput("smooth", label = "Add smoother?", # add smoother
    value = FALSE)
),

conditionalPanel(
  condition = "input.theTabs == 'animated'",
  sliderInput("animation", "Trend over time",
    min = 0, max = 80, value = 0, step = 5,
    animate = animationOptions(interval = 1000, loop = TRUE)
  )
)
```

As you can see, the condition appears very R/Shiny-like, except with the `.` operator familiar to JavaScript users in place of `$`. This is a very simple but powerful way of making sure that your UI is not cluttered with irrelevant material.

Beautiful tables with DataTable

The latest version of Shiny has added support to draw tables using the wonderful DataTables jQuery library. This will enable your users to search and sort through large tables very easily. To see DataTable in action, visit the homepage at `http://datatables.net/` or run the application featured in this chapter. The version in this application summarizes the values of different variables across the different countries from which browser hits originate and looks as follows:

The package can be installed using `install.packages("DT")` and needs to be loaded in the preamble to the `server.R` file with `library(DT)`. Once this is done, using the package is quite straightforward. There are two functions: one in `server.R` (`renderDataTable`) and one in `ui.R` (`dataTableOutput`). They are used as following:

```
### server. R
output$countryTable <- DT::renderDataTable ({
  groupCountry <- group_by(passData(), country)
  groupByCountry <- summarise(groupCountry,
    meanSession =
    mean(sessionDuration),
    users = log(sum(users)),
    sessions = log(sum(sessions))
  )
  datatable(groupByCountry)
})

### ui.R
tabPanel("Table", DT::dataTableOutput("countryTable"),
  value = "table")
```

Anything that returns a dataframe or a matrix can be used within `renderDataTable()`.

Note that as of Shiny V. 0.12, the Shiny functions, `renderDataTable()` and `dataTableOutput()`, are deprecated: you should use the DT equivalents of the same name, as in the preceding code, adding DT:: before each function name specifies that the function should be drawn from that package.

Reactive user interfaces

Another trick you will definitely want up your sleeve at some point is a reactive user interface. This enables you to change your UI (for example, the number or content of radio buttons) based on reactive functions.

For example, consider an application that I wrote related to survey responses across a broad range of health services in different areas. The services are related to each other in quite a complex hierarchy, and over time, different areas and services respond (or cease to exist, or merge, or change their name), which means that for each time period, the user might be interested in, there would be a totally different set of areas and services. The only sensible solution to this problem is to have the user tell you which area and date range they are interested in and then give them back the correct list of services that have survey responses within that area and date range.

The example we're going to look at is a little simpler than this, just to keep from getting bogged down in too much detail, but the principle is exactly the same and you should not find this idea too difficult to adapt to your own UI. We are going to allow users to constrain their data by the country of origin of the browser hit. Although we could design the UI by simply taking all the countries that exist in the entire dataset and placing them all in a combo box to be selected, it is a lot cleaner to only allow the user to select from the countries that are actually present within the particular date range they have selected.

This has the added advantage of preventing the user from selecting any countries of origin, which do not have any browser hits within the currently selected dataset. In order to do this, we are going to create a reactive user interface, that is, one that changes based on data values, which come about from user input.

The reactive user interface example – server.R

When you are making a reactive user interface, the big difference is that instead of writing your UI definition in your `ui.R` file, you place it in `server.R`, and wrap it in `renderUI()`. Then, all you do is point to it from your `ui.R` file.

Let's take a look at the relevant bit of the `server.R` file:

```
output$reactCountries <- renderUI({
  countryList = unique(as.character(passData()$country))
  selectInput("theCountries", "Choose country", countryList)
})
```

The first line takes the reactive dataset that contains only the data between the dates selected by the user and gives all the unique values of countries within it. The second line is a widget type we have not used yet that generates a combo box. The usual `id` and `label` arguments are given, followed by the values that the combo box can take. This is taken from the variable defined in the first line.

The reactive user interface example – ui.R

The `ui.R` file merely needs to point to the reactive definition, as shown in the following line of code (just add it in to the list of widgets within `sidebarPanel()`):

```
uiOutput("reactCountries")
```

You can now point to the value of the widget in the usual way, as `input$subDomains`. Note that you do not use the name as defined in the call to `renderUI()`, that is, `reactCountries`, but rather the name as defined within it, that is, `theCountries`.

Progress bars

It is quite common within Shiny applications and in analytics generally, to have computations or data fetches that take a long time. Later in the chapter, you will learn some of the ways in which you can control the reactive relationships within an application in order to reduce unnecessary processing.

However, even using all these tools, it will sometimes be necessary for the user to wait some time before their output is returned. In cases like this, it is a good practice to do two things: first, to inform that the server is processing the request and has not simply crashed or otherwise failed, and second, to give the user some idea of how much time has elapsed because they requested the output and how much time they have remaining to wait.

This is achieved very simply in Shiny using the `withProgress()` function. This function defaults to measuring progress on a scale from 0 to 1 and produces a loading bar at the top of the application with the information from the `message` and `detail` arguments of the loading function.

You can refer to the following code that the `withProgress` function is used to wrap a function (in this case, the function that draws the map), with message and detail arguments describing what has happened and an initial value of 0 (value = 0, that is, no progress yet):

```
withProgress(message = 'Please wait',
  detail = 'Drawing map...', value = 0, {
  ... function code...
})
```

As the code is stepped through, the value of progress can steadily be increased from 0 to 1 (for example, in a `for()` loop) using:

```
incProgress(1/3)
```

The third time this is called the value of progress will be 1, which indicates that the function has completed (although other values of progress can be selected where necessary, see `?withProgess()`). To summarize, the finished code looks as follows:

```
withProgress(message = 'Please wait',
  detail = 'Drawing map...', value = 0, {
  ... function code...
  incProgress(1/3)
  ... function code...
  incProgress(1/3)
  ... function code...
  incProgress(1/3)
})
```

It's as simple as that. Again, take a look at the application to see it in action. If you need to give your user more detailed information about how far they are through the processing, the `incProgress()` function also takes a message argument, which will append that message to the overall **Please wait** message already given by `withProgress()`. For example, you may wish to write `incProgress(1/3, message = "Summarizing data")`, perhaps `incProgress(1/3, message = "Generating graph")`, and so on.

Advanced reactivity and data handling

Now that we've warmed up a bit, let's discuss loading data and reactivity in a bit more detail. The first thing to note is the different ways to load data in R and the effects each has. Data can be loaded before the `shinyServer()` function, within the `shinyServer()` function, or within a reactive function, which is itself defined within `shinyServer()`.

Each has a different effect. Data loaded outside the `shinyServer()` function will be loaded once only, whenever the Shiny server instance is launched (for more on running your own Shiny server see *Chapter 7, Sharing Your Creations*). When you're running programs locally, the server instance is launched every time the program is launched, so for local applications, there is no difference between this and data loaded within the `shinyServer()` call.

When running on a real server, however, the server will be launched once and left running for months. As a consequence, this first method is a good place to perform very heavy, long running data fetch and processing operations which they will run very infrequently. Data loading and processing carried out within the `shinyServer()` function will be run every time a new instance launches. Again, when running locally this is not different to functions outside of the `shinyServer()` call, but, on a server, code placed here will run every time a new user visits the web page. This is a good place, therefore, to carry out processing that the user will not mind waiting for as the page loads but does not necessarily want to sit through as they use the application. Finally, there are data loading functions that run within reactive functions inside a `shinyServer()` call.

As you already learned, reactive functions and objects automatically take dependencies on their inputs. We also saw that it's often a good idea to use reactive objects rather than just output functions because data objects can be created once and then passed around to different output functions.

We're now going to discuss in a bit more detail, the use of reactive objects in Shiny as well as special functions within it to control reactivity. There is more about reactivity and some very helpful diagrams on the Shiny tutorial pages at shiny. rstudio.com/articles/reactivity-overview.html.

The default approach to reactivity in Shiny, as we have seen throughout the book, handles quite a lot of different scenarios quite well. However, sometimes, the default behavior will be slow or confusing for users of your application or will result in code that is hard to write or maintain or even just not useful. Along with using reactive objects within Shiny, there are special functions that you can use to take control of inputs and outputs to Shiny applications. I'll summarize them briefly and then show some use cases for each one within the Google Analytics application.

The `submitButton()` and `isolate()` functions are both used in cases where data is slow to get or process. In essence, they allow you to control when Shiny processes information from a dependency. So, for example, if your data processing instruction takes 10 seconds to run, users won't mind waiting a few times, but they don't want to wait every time they click on a button.

The `submitButton()` function controls the whole interface, and no reactive processing is carried out until it has been pushed by the user. The `isolate()` function is a little more subtle than this and allows you to prevent reactive objects and functions from forming dependencies on individual inputs. Essentially, it prevents a costly rerun of data processing or output every time irrelevant changes are made on the UI and gives a smoother experience for your user.

Another weapon in your reactivity arsenal is `invalidateLater()`, which allows you to make an object reactive, not on the basis of user inputs but rather on the passing of time. An obvious example would be a financial information application, which is refreshed every minute on a server to which the application has access. The outputs can be kept up to date even when the user is not interacting with the application using the `invalidateLater()` function.

Let's take a closer look at each of these methods in turn.

Controlling the whole interface with submitButton()

This is easily the simplest approach to dealing with a lot of the problems that you might encounter with slow reactive functions. The submitButton() function allows you to include a button on your UI, which ensures that no functions run at all until the button is clicked. The same reactive dependencies are taken by output functions, so the programming is just as simple, but the users can take their time selecting the right inputs before the long computation for the outputs begins. Place the following into a UI definition:

```
submitButton(text = "Produce output")
```

That's it! Although a wonderfully simple method, in some circumstances, it would be an overkill and takes away the feeling of interactivity even when the user is making minor changes to the output (the title of a graph, for example). Shiny does give you finer control than this, should you need it. This is achieved with the isolate() function.

Controlling specific inputs with the isolate() function

The isolate() function allows you to take particular parts of the input and break the dependency that they would otherwise form with reactive functions. Within our application, the map plotting function takes a long time to execute, and so, it is a good idea to avoid refreshing it every time a minor change is made to the data.

For example, to change the date range, the user will make two selections – the date at which the user wants the data selection to begin and the date at which the user wants the data selection to terminate. It is a waste of server processing time to redraw the map based on the first of these selections because it will need to be redrawn when the second date selection is made.

We can add a dependency to a button, which can then be used to update the map when the user has finished selecting their data very simply using the actionButton() function. The action button is defined very simply in the UI, as follows:

```
actionButton("drawMap", "Update map")
```

The two arguments, as usual, give the name of the input and a label for it. Within the `server.R` file, the code is as follows:

```
output$ggplotMap <- renderPlot ({
  input$drawMap # dependency on actionButton
  if (length (unique (as.character (passData ()$country))) < 2) {
    return ()
  }
```

These first two lines establish the dependency on the action button, which we have already described, and ensure that there are at least two countries within the dataset. Only having one country in the data (which can happen over very narrow date ranges) causes the code to crash.

Testing conditions and using `return ()` to break out of a function is a very effective way of avoiding crashes in Shiny and can be particularly useful in a lot of applications, which will generate error messages until long running reactive functions return values, at which point they will run successfully. Using `return ()` in this way is a very quick way of sparing your user the confusion of reading error messages which then disappear once all the code in the application has executed.

In this specific case, it might be a good idea to print a warning as to why nothing has been returned or to perhaps change the inputs to valid selections, but we will not be detained by this here; pop-up widgets using JavaScript or jQuery are covered in *Chapter 3, Building Your Own Web Pages with Shiny*.

```
groupCountry <- isolate ( # avoid dependency on data
  group_by (passData (), country)
)
```

Here, we can look at the first data instruction, which would otherwise form a dependency on the reactive dataset is wrapped in `isolate ()`.

The remainder of the code draws the map; this has been covered in *Chapter 2, Building Your First Application*.

Running reactive functions over time

Another way of controlling reactivity within your application is the `invalidateLater ()` command. The `invalidateLater ()` command causes reactive functions to re-execute after a certain period of time has elapsed. This function is used a lot in real-time applications, such as stock market analysis tools.

Note that the `invalidateLater()` function takes a `session` argument. This is used in some of Shiny's advanced functions. Simply give the `shinyServer()` call a session argument (`shinyServer(function(input, output, session) {`) and then add in the argument wherever necessary in the rest of your code. The documentation (can be found by entering `?shiny` at the console. As a reminder, accessing help files this way is represented in this book simply as `?shiny`, `?ggplot`, and so on) will make clear which functions require a session argument. Many of the advanced functions within Shiny make use of this argument.

The other argument that `invalidateLater()` takes is the number of milliseconds you wish to elapse before the function is called again. One only needs to place `invalidateLater(10000, session)` within any reactive function, and it will be re-evaluated every time the specified time elapses. Note that when you use `invalidateLater()`, you must put all other dependencies in `isolate()`; otherwise, it will re-execute both when the time elapses or when the inputs change.

Using reactive objects and functions efficiently

As we saw, using a reactive object is a good idea to save from having to maintain several chunks of code that all do the same thing (typically, prepare your data based on user inputs). Another time you might want to use reactive objects is if your reactive function is inefficient or slow.

Sometimes, a reactive object is a good idea if you have a lot of complicated inputs that need coercing to different variable types; it's easier to produce a nice, clean, and simple R object with all the correct variable types in it than to write lots of horrible `as.character(input$variable)` calls all over the place and remember in what variable type everything is.

So, for example, I did some fiddling with the output of the widgets to build the widget browser presented in *Chapter 2, Building Your First Application*, in order to fit all the different output types in one column (browse back to *Chapter 2, Building Your First Application*, to take a look, use `runGist(6571951)` to run the application, or refer to `https://gist.github.com/ChrisBeeley/6571951` for the code). This was fine for this one example, but if I had needed the output elsewhere in the application again, I certainly would not like to write and maintain code to remake it from the inputs every time.

It is much easier to just build the object once, place it in a reactive object and then call on it wherever you need it.

More advanced topics in Shiny

The remainder of this chapter will be spent looking at some of the other functions that Shiny includes that can give your users a smoother and well-featured experience.

Finely controlling inputs and outputs

Shiny offers a variety of functions that allow you to directly control the user interface. You can program functions that take direct control over any of the input widgets, changing their labels, input range, or current selection, as well as switching the tabs on a `tabsetPanel()`-based UI, all using built-in functions. The following example uses `updateCheckboxGroupInput()`, which, as its name implies, is used to update the parameters of a `checkboxGroupInput()`-based widget. We also need the `observe()` function to make it work.

The `observe()` function is for reactive functions that do not return objects but rather are run for their effect—controlling parts of the user interface, creating files, and so on. In this example, we are going to use it to control the UI, but don't forget that it can be used for lots of other purposes.

Let's see how they both work together to achieve the desired effect. Without controlling the checkboxes, which choose the network domain of interest, we expose the user to the risk that they will make an invalid selection. If they select just the NHS domain and then draw a map, the function will always fail because, by definition, all domain traffic from the NHS comes from within the United Kingdom.

It's useful, therefore, to ensure that when the map is selected, this particular selection is not possible (perhaps with a note on the interface, so the user does not think the application is bugged). This is achieved very simply for this checkbox group as follows:

```
# control the checkboxes when the map is selected
observe({
  if(input$theTabs == "map"){
    updateCheckboxGroupInput(session, "domainShow",
      choices = list("NHS users" =
        "nhs.uk",
        "Other" = "Other"),
      selected = c("nhs.uk", "Other")
    )
  }
})
```

As can be seen, the code checks to see if the map is selected and if it is, automatically selects both boxes for network domain. Note that `updateCheckboxGroupInput()` also takes a session argument. Other than that extra detail, the `updateCheckboxGroupInput()` function is very simple to use and allows you to completely redraw the widget—so you could, in theory, add or take away options as well.

A nice side effect of controlling the UI like this is that we now don't have to test elsewhere for valid inputs. Controlling user inputs so that they are always valid can be a useful way of writing clean and simple code and letting your users know what is and isn't possible at the same time.

In the following example, we will use `observe()` again for a more advanced purpose, that is, controlling the user interface based on the URL, which the user uses to access the server.

Reading client information and GET requests in Shiny

Shiny includes some very useful functionality that allows you to read information from a client's web browser, such as information from the URL (including GET search requests), size of plots in pixels, and so on.

All you need to do, as before, is run `shinyServer()` with a `session` argument. This causes, among other things, an object to be created that holds information about a client's session named `session$clientData`.

The exact content of this object will depend on what is open on the screen. The following objects will always exist:

```
url_hostname     # hostname, e.g. localhost or chrisbeeley.net
url_pathname =   # path, e.g. / or /shiny
url_port =       # port number (8100 for localhost, can optionally
                 # change when hosting, see chapter 5)
url_protocol =   # highly likely to be http:
url_search =     # the text after the "?" in the URL. In the
following
                 # example this will read "?person=NHS&smooth=yes".
```

Different output types will yield different information. Plots will give the following information, among other return values:

```
output_myplot_height = # in pixels
output_myplot_width =  # in pixels
```

There are many applications to which this information can be put, such as giving different UIs or default settings to users from different domains, or configuring graphs and other outputs based on their size (for example, for users who are using mobile devices or 32" monitors). We're going to look at perhaps the most obvious and powerful use of client data: the search string.

Custom interfaces from GET strings

In this example, we're going to produce URLs that allow Shiny to configure itself when the user lands at the page to save them from having to set up their preferences each time. We will make use of two variables: one specifies that a user is only interested in data from the NHS network domain and the other specifies that the user wants a smoothing line present on their trend graph. Users who request a smoothing line will also be taken straight to the trendline tab.

As well as the work with the GET query, the only extra bit we will need here is a function to change the selected panel from a tabsetPanel(). This is done, unsurprisingly, using the updateTabsetPanel() command.

Catering for these different needs is very easily done by creating URLs that encode the preferences and giving them to the different users. To simplify the code, we will pretend that, if they are passed at all, the correct number of search terms is always passed in the correct order. This is a reasonable assumption if you write the URLs yourself. In a real-world example, the URLs are most likely going to be generated programmatically from a UI. Correctly parsing them is not too challenging, but it is not really the focus of the discussion here. The following are the two URLs we will give out:

- feedbacksite.nhs.uk/shiny?person=NHS&smooth=yes
- feedbacksite.nhs.uk/shiny?person=other&smooth=no

As in the previous example, the code is wrapped in observe(), and the first portion of the code returns the search terms from the URL as a named list:

```
observe({
  searchString <- parseQueryString(session$clientData$url_search)
  ...
```

Having done this, we can then check that a `searchString` exists (in case other users land from the default URL) and, if it does, change the settings accordingly. The `updateTabsetPanel()` command uses a lot of the concepts we already saw when we read the tab that was selected. The function takes a `session` argument, an `inputId` argument (the name of the panel), and a `selected` argument (the name of the tab):

```
# update inputs according to query string
if(length(searchString) > 0){ # if the searchString exists

  # deal with first query which indicates the audience
  if(searchString[[1]] == "nhs"){ # for NHS users do the following
    updateCheckboxGroupInput(session, "domainShow",
      choices = list("NHS users" = "nhs.uk",
      "Other" = "Other"), selected = c("nhs.uk"))
  }

  # do they want a smooth?
  if(searchString[[2]] == "yes"){
    updateTabsetPanel(session, "theTabs", selected = "trend")
    updateCheckboxInput(session, inputId = "smooth",
      value = TRUE)
  }
}
})
```

This is clearly a very powerful way to make the experience better for your users completely transparently. You may wish to spend a bit of time setting up a web interface in whatever language you like (PHP, JavaScript, and so on) and correctly parsing the URLs that you generate within Shiny. If you need to handle varying lengths and names of lists, you will need a few extra commands:

- `names(theList)`: This will give you the name of each return value
- `length(unlist(theList))`: This will tell you how long the list is

Advanced graphics options

Although `renderPlot()` makes it very easy to produce reactive outputs, as we've seen, it only works with the standard method of outputting graphics in R. Images from certain packages within R as well as images created outside of R will not be displayed.

Helpfully, Shiny includes a function to render all image files within a Shiny application: `renderImage()`. The simplest case is where you have a prerendered image that you wish to include. In the `server.R` file, the `renderImage()` call is made, returning a list with the path to the image and optionally the content type (to save Shiny from having to guess based on the file extension):

```
output$imageFile <- renderImage({
   list(src = "foo.png", contentType = "image/png")
}, deleteFile = FALSE)
```

The `deleteFile` argument is set to `false`; otherwise, the file will be removed after display. This is intended for when the image is generated within the call. The file is no longer needed, so it can be deleted after the image is displayed.

Finally, the `ui.R` just includes the following:

```
imageOutput("imageFile")
```

Downloading graphics and reports

The option to download graphics and reports can be added easily using `downloadHandler()`. Essentially, `downloadHandler()` has two arguments that both contain functions—one to define the path to which the download should go and one that defines what is to be downloaded.

The first thing we need to do is take any functions that are used either in the download graphic request or the report and make them reactive functions, which can be called from anywhere rather than instructions to draw a graph within a call to `renderPlot()`. The effect of this, of course, is that we only have one function to write and maintain rather than one inside the download graphic function, one inside the download report function, and so on. This is achieved very simply like this:

```
trendGraph <- reactive({
   ... rest of function that was inside renderPlot
})
```

The graph can now very easily be printed within the trend tab like this:

```
output$trend <- renderPlot({
   trendGraph()
})
```

We'll go through the following code from `server.R` step by step:

```
output$downloadData.trend <- downloadHandler(
  filename <- function() {
    paste("Trend_plot", Sys.Date(),".png",sep="")
  },
```

This is the `filename` function, and as you can see, it produces a filename `Trend_plot_XX_.png` where XX is the current date:

```
content <- function(file) {
  png(file, width = 980, height = 400,
    units = "px", pointsize = 12,
    bg = "white", res = NA)
  trend.plot <- trendGraph()
  print(trend.plot)
  dev.off()
},
```

This is the `content` function, and as you can see, it opens a png device (`?png`), calls a reactive function named `myTrend()`, which draws the graph, prints to the device, and closes with a call to `dev.off()`. You can set up the `trendGraph()` function very simply; in this case, it is just like the function that draws the graph itself except instead of being wrapped in `renderPlot()` to indicate that it is a Shiny output that is just defined as a reactive function.

Finally, the following is given to tell Shiny what type of file to expect:

```
  contentType = 'image/png')
```

Adding the download button to the `ui.R` file is simple; the `downloadButton()` function takes the name of the download handler as defined in `server.R` and a label for the button:

```
tabPanel("Trend", plotOutput("trend"),
  downloadButton("downloadData.trend", "Download graphic")
```

As you can see, I have added the button underneath the graph, so users know what they are downloading.

Downloadable reports with knitr

This same function can very easily allow your users to produce custom reports in HTML, pdf, or MS Word ready to be downloaded to their machines, using the knitr package (http://yihui.name/knitr/). Knitr is a user-contributed package that allows reports to be generated dynamically from a mixture of a static report format interleaved with the output from R.

So, for example, titles and text can be fixed, but each time the report is run, different outputs will be produced within the document depending on the state of the data when the output is generated. Knitr can be used with the RMarkdown format described in *Chapter 2, Building Your First Application*. Here is the simple RMarkdown document within the Google Analytics application:

```
# Summary report
## Text summary
This report summarises data between `r strftime(input$dateRange[1],
    format = "%d %B %Y")` and `r strftime(input$dateRange[2],
    format = "%d %B %Y")`.


## Trend graph
```{r fig.width=7, fig.height=6, echo=FALSE}
trendGraph()
```
```

As can be seen, the document is a mix of static headings and text, inline R output (given as `` `r "print("somthing")` ``, and graphical output (chunks of code, as we saw in *Chapter 2, Building Your First Application*, being demarcated with `` ```{r ... }``` ``. The `trendGraph()` function, of course, is the same `trendGraph()` function that we saw in the download graphics code.

The code to download the report is simply as follows (with the RMarkdown document in the same folder as `server.R` and named `"Report.Rmd"`):

```
output$downloadDoc <-
    downloadHandler(filename = "Report.html",
      content = function(file){
        knit2html("Report.Rmd", envir = environment())

        # copy document to 'file'
        file.copy("Report.html", file,
          overwrite = TRUE)
      }
    )
```

Adding a button to download the graph is the same as for the downloading graph function; the following should be placed in `ui.R` within the `sidebarPanel()` function:

```
downloadButton("downloadDoc", "Download report")
```

Downloading and uploading data

Downloading data is done in a very similar fashion, which looks like the following `downloadHandler()` call:

```
output$downloadData <- downloadHandler(
  filename = function(){
    "myData.csv"
  }
  content = function(file){
    write.csv(passData(), file)
  }
)
```

Uploading data is achieved using the `fileInput()` function. In the following example, we will assume that the user wishes to upload a comma-separated spreadsheet (`.csv`) file. The button is added to `ui.R` in the following manner:

```
fileInput("uploadFile", "Upload your own CSV file")
```

This button allows a user to select their own `.csv` file, and it also makes a variety of objects based on the ID (in this case, `input$uploadFile$...`) available from `server.R`. The most useful is `input$uploadFile$datapath`, which is a path to the file itself and can be turned into a dataframe using `read.csv()`:

```
userData <- read.csv(input$uploadFile$datapath)
```

There are other bits of information about the file available. Take a look at `?fileInput` for more details.

Debugging

Debugging Shiny applications can be a bit tricky at times. Unlike many analytics applications, using R outputs cannot be stepped through simply, and sometimes, error messages can be a little difficult to understand. Shiny does have some quite useful debugging functions, and there are some sensible practices to be used whenever you write Shiny code that should help you to avoid too many problems with debugging.

Good practice when coding Shiny applications

Probably, the most effective weapon in your armory when you are trying to write bug-free code that is easy to maintain is always making sure that anything you write within Shiny will also run outside of Shiny. You would be amazed how often this rule is violated in forum questions. Error messages can often be obscure, and fixing your code based on the messages that Shiny brings back can often be futile. Break the offending piece of code out of the Shiny application and ensure that it works in a standard interactive R call.

Once you're confident that you've run a few test cases outside of Shiny and they run as you would expect, the next step is to simplify your Shiny application. A complex chain of functions control reactivity within your application; breaking and creating dependencies could easily be the source of the problem and not the function you are trying to fix. Write a minimal Shiny application with minimal data processing and a minimal set of outputs and verify that it works. Build out from here until you reproduce the problem.

A further advantage of this approach is that you now have the perfect code to write a forum post to get help on Stack Exchange or similar. Show the code that works and the line or chunk that breaks the code as well as the error message. This should generate useful responses from experts on the forum.

Debugging functions

Along with a good practice with coding and seeking help on forums, you can also use Shiny's debugging functions, which are much improved from earlier versions of Shiny. They are described in detail at `shiny.rstudio.com/articles/debugging.html`. The most valuable of these is not strictly a specialized debugging function but rather a standard function within R. Wherever you want to find out the state of variables in a Shiny application, just include the following line:

```
cat(... variable of interest...)
```

This will print the value of the variable (you may need to cast it to something that can be handled by `cat()`, for example, `cat(as.numeric(input$title))`. This will run throughout as the data values within the application change, which makes it very valuable to see exactly what is happening at different stages. And, of course, you can move the `cat()` function around or have several to get a very detailed account of what is happening within the application.

Another useful standard R function is `browser()`, which will stop the execution and switch to debug mode as soon as it is called. R options can also be set to choose between a call to `browser()` and `recover()` when an error occurs by using `options(error = browser)` or `options(error = recover)` (for more on these functions, take a look at `?browser` and `?recover`).

Similarly, options can be set to determine Shiny's error handling using `options(shiny.error = browser)`. Calling `options(shiny.trace = TRUE)` prints all messages between the server and client to the console, which is very useful in order to get detailed information about where the code is going wrong.

Summary

In this chapter, you saw most of the functionality within Shiny. It's a relatively small but powerful toolbox with which you can build a vast array of useful and intuitive applications with comparatively little effort. In this respect, ggplot2 is rather a good companion for Shiny because it too offers you a fairly limited selection of functions with which knowledgeable users can very quickly build many different graphical outputs.

In this chapter, we looked at fine-tuning the UI using `conditionalPanel()` and `observe()` and changing your UI reactively. We also looked at managing slow computations using Shiny's reactivity functions, customizing a user's experience using client data, custom graphics, animation and reports, and uploading and downloading data. Finally, we looked at the sometimes difficult world of debugging Shiny applications.

In the next two chapters, we are going to build some more applications to make you learn more about the power of Shiny. The first application is a dashboard, and we will concentrate on layout and styling and how to make large applications smooth and intuitive. In the second application, we will use JavaScript, D3, and other tools to enhance the interactivity of our Shiny applications.

5

Advanced Applications I – Dashboards

This chapter is all about laying out your Shiny applications. In *Chapter 3, Building Your Own Web Pages with Shiny*, we already looked at doing it by hand, using HTML or CSS, and we already saw how to lay out multiple output windows using `tabsetPanel()`. Shiny (and its associated packages) includes loads of functions that allow you to lay out your applications beautifully and simply. This chapter takes the code and applications you have already seen and takes them from the very plain, vanilla-looking layout that the default styling returns to slick, customizable layouts, culminating in your very own Google Analytics dashboard.

In this chapter, we will do the following things:

- Revise the basics of layout in Shiny applications and look at simple ways of extending the basic layout functions
- Add icons to the applications
- Learn about the bootstrap layout functions, which enable you to very easily lay applications out using a grid
- Change the look and feel of an application using menu bars
- Build a dashboard to help your users access all the information they need from within the same intuitive interface

Applications in this chapter

In order to better understand the layout functions in particular, we're not going to add any functionality in this chapter. We'll start off with the vanilla Google Analytics application we saw in *Chapter 2, Building Your First Application*, and will apply different types of layout to it, so you can see how they work. As we progress, we will add one or two extra features (querying client data from the browser and another type of map). However, we will mainly focus on looking at the same application but with different types of layout function applied to it.

It is highly recommended that you download and run all the code in this chapter, so you can get a better sense of how the applications work as well as seeing the server.R code in each case, which won't be repeated for each application. If you're not in front of a computer while you are reading this section, hopefully, there are enough screenshots and explanatory material to keep you going until you can see the applications in action for yourself.

Version one – sidebar layout

We'll start off slow with the vanilla sidebar layout, just to establish the building blocks of our dashboard. Because we're not doing too much in the way of features or layout in this first application, we'll add a few visual bells and whistles. Some of them will be dropped in later versions of the application just to stop the code and UI from becoming too cluttered, but you can of course write an application yourself with all of the UI elements in if you wish so. All of the code and data for the applications in this chapter is available at chrisbeeley.net/website/.

Adding icons to your UI

As we go through the various UI elements later, we're going to sprinkle a few icons throughout, just to give the page a bit more visual interest. Icons can come from two icon libraries, located at fontawesome.io/icons/ and getbootstrap.com/components/#glyphicons. They can be added simply using the icon() command with the name of the required icon given as a string.

For example, icon("user") will by default return icons from the fontawesome library, and to use the glyphicons, simply add lib = "glyphicon" as follows:

```
icon = icon("user", lib = "glyphicon")
```

They can be added directly to your UI or on buttons (including the buttons at the top of tab panels). From the full code of this application, you can see that we have replaced the boring horizontal rule, which separated our input widgets with a spinning Linux penguin (because, woo! Linux!) using `class = "fa-spin"`. The `class` argument comes from the use of CSS classes to vary the characteristics of Font Awesome icons. The examples are given at `fortawesome.github.io/Font-Awesome/examples/`. You can alter the size of font awesome icons with `class = "fa-lg"` (one-third larger) `class = "fa-2x"`, (twice as large) `class = "fa-3x"`, up to `class = "fa-5x"`.

Putting them together, we get the following:

```
icon("linux", class = "fa-spin fa-3x")
```

There are icons added to an action button and a tab panel below, so look out for them in the code following.

Using shinyBS to add pop-ups and tooltips

The first thing we're going to look at is using the shinyBS package to add pop-up windows and tooltips. There is more on the functionality of the shinyBS package present at `cran.r-project.org/web/packages/shinyBS/shinyBS.pdf`. If you haven't installed already, install shinyBS with `install.packages("shinyBS")`.

The `server.R` file is very similar to the version we encountered in *Chapter 2, Building Your First Application*, except the map that has been removed (this will be added back in later on in the chapter), and there are a couple of more functions to power the new UI elements.

The first changes are visible at the top of `server.R`; we are using the shinyBS package:

```
...[load packages from original application]...
library(shinyBS)
```

Also, `shinyServer()` takes a session argument:

```
shinyServer(function(input, output, session){
```

We saw the use of the session argument in *Chapter 3, Building Your Own Web Pages with Shiny*; in this case, it will be used for two purposes: first, to collect data from the client about the size of plots and, second, as an argument to some of the functions in the shinyBS package, which we will be using in this application.

We will now use the `session` argument to collect data about the session:

```
# function from shiny.rstudio.com/articles/client-data.html
cdata <- session$clientData

# Values from cdata returned as text
output$clientdataText <- renderText({
  cnames <- names(cdata)
  allvalues <- lapply(cnames, function(name) {
    paste(name, cdata[[name]], sep=" = ")
  })
  paste(allvalues, collapse = "\n")
})
```

This data will be shown with a nice pop-up like this:

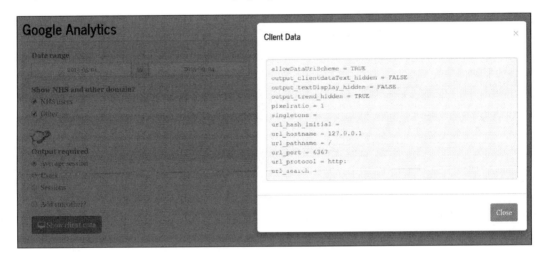

This is achieved using shinyBS in the `ui.R` file. Let's head there now.

ui.R

The `ui.R` file is also pretty similar to the one we encountered in *Chapter 2, Building Your First Application*. We're going to add two controls to the sidebar by adding them in as arguments to `sidebarPanel()`:

```
sidebarPanel(
  ...[controls from chapter two version]...
  actionButton("showData", "Show client data",
    icon = icon("desktop")),
  bsTooltip(id = "domainShow",
    title = "Deselecting both sources will default to all data",
    placement = "right")
)
```

The bsTooltip is a handy one-liner, it adds a hover (by default, or you can choose a different trigger) tooltip to any UI element. In this case, we have passed id = "domainShow", which refers to the two checkboxes that select network traffic from the NHS domain and/or all other domains. The other two arguments give the contents of the tooltip and its placement relative to the control, respectively.

Now to add a pop-up window in the main output area, we are going to add a call to the bsModal() function within tabsetPanel():

```
tabsetPanel( # set up tabbed output
  tabPanel("Summary", textOutput("textDisplay"),
    icon = icon("user",
      lib = "glyphicon")
  ),
  tabPanel("Trend", plotOutput("trend"),
    icon = icon("calendar")
  ),
  bsModal(id = "clientData",
    title = "Client Data", trigger = "showData",
    verbatimTextOutput("clientdataText")
  )
)
```

The bsModal() function takes an id and title argument, as with many Shiny functions. As you can see, the trigger is defined as showData, which is the ID of the action button, which we already added to the sidebar in the preceding code.

Finally, we give the output of the function, which is the text output we already set up in server.R (output$clientdataText). Clicking the button now brings up a pop-up window with the entire client data printed within it.

Adding a pop-up window to an output

The `addPopover()` function from the `shinyBS()` package allows you to add pop-up windows to input or output elements within a shiny application. This is another one-liner, back in the `server.R` file, along with the function that draws the graph:

```
output$trend <- renderPlot({
  ...[functions from previous chapter]...
  if(input$smooth){
    thePlot <- thePlot + geom_smooth()
  }
  print(thePlot)
  addPopover(session, id = "trend", title = "Source",
    content = "All data from Google Analyics website at <a href =
    'http://example.com'>http://example.com</a>",
    trigger = 'click')
})
```

As you can see, `addPopover()` takes the session argument, which we gave to `shinyServer()` at the top, along with the ID of the element that we wish to annotate (`trend`) and a title (`Source`). Raw HTML can be passed straight in as in the preceding example.

Using shinythemes

Let's give the whole application a lick of paint using the shinythemes package. If you haven't already, install it with `install.packages("shinythemes")`. The documentation (including a list of the available themes) can be found at `rstudio. github.io/shinythemes/`. Load the package and pass a theme into `fluidPage()`:

```
library(shinythemes)
shinyUI(fluidPage(theme = shinytheme("journal"),
  ... rest of UI...
```

Enjoy your new theme and consult the documentation for the other available themes and the appearance of each.

And here's the finished application:

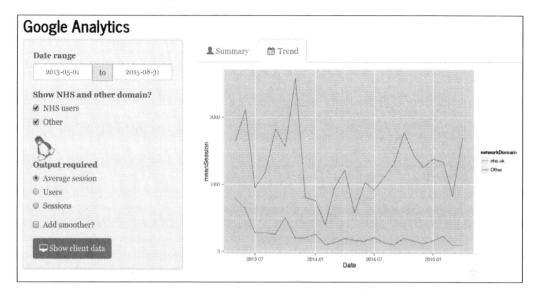

It's very simple, if you prefer, to use a navlist down the side of the application and organize some or all of your input widgets and your output widgets like that.

There follows a screenshot of this same application redone using a navlist with two of the outputs shown. In the real application, you obviously have to click on the buttons on the left to get these different views. Note that the date has been left outside of the navlist, which means that the date is visible in all states of the application:

The code is very similar to the previously mentioned code, except the fact that input and output elements are all arranged in a navlist as follows:

```
library(shiny)
library(shinythemes)
library(shinyBS)

shinyUI(fluidPage(theme = shinytheme("journal"),
  titlePanel("Google Analytics"),
  dateRangeInput(inputId = "dateRange", label = "Date range",
    start - "2013-05-01"),
  navlistPanel(
    tabPanel("Inputs",
      checkboxGroupInput(...[as above]...),
      radioButtons(...[as above]...),
      checkboxInput(...[as above]...),
      actionButton(...[as above]...),
      bsTooltip(...[as above]...)
    ),
    tabPanel("Summary", textOutput("textDisplay")),
    tabPanel("Trend", plotOutput("trend"),
      icon = icon("calendar")),
    bsModal(id = "clientData", title = "Client Data",
      trigger = "showData",
      verbatimTextOutput("clientdataText")
    )
  )
)
```

Version two – grid layout (A)

In the next version of the application, we're going to use the `fluidRow()` function to apply a custom layout to the UI. This function allows you to implement the standard bootstrap grid layout, as described at `w3schools.com/bootstrap/bootstrap_grid_system.asp`.

The width of the screen is given as 12 units, and you can pass the `column()` functions of arbitrary size into a `fluidRow()` instruction to define a group of widths adding up to 12. In this simple example, we will have three columns within the first row and then one in the second row. The finished application looks like this:

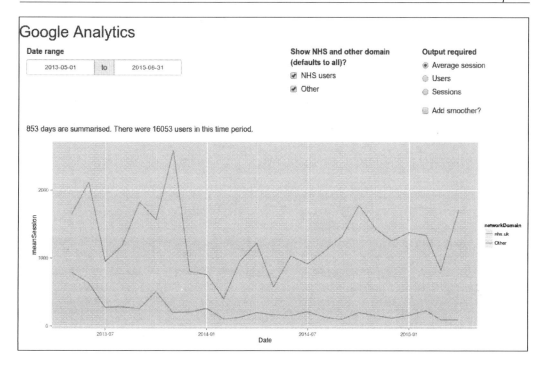

ui.R

Let's look at the `ui.R` file necessary to achieve this. The `server.R` file remains the same as in the previous example. We'll take breaks as we step through the code to understand what's happening:

```
library(shiny)
shinyUI(fluidPage(
  # Application title
  titlePanel("Google Analytics"),
```

We start with `titlePanel()`, as in the previous application.

```
fluidRow(
```

Now we add in rows of UI elements using the `fluidRow()` function:

```
column(6,
  dateRangeInput(inputId = "dateRange",
  label = "Date range",
  start = "2013-05-01")
),
```

Each `fluidRow()` instruction comprises a number of `column()` functions that contain a width (the widths of all columns totaling 12) and a UI element. In this case, you can see the width is 6 (half of the screen) and the date range widget:

```
column(3, checkboxGroupInput(inputId = "domainShow",
  label = "Show NHS and other domain
  (defaults to all)?",
  choices = list("NHS users" = "nhs.uk",
    "Other" = "Other"),
  selected = c("nhs.uk", "Other")
)),

column(3, radioButtons(inputId = "outputRequired",
  label = "Output required",
  choices = list("Average session" = "meanSession",
    "Users" = "users",
    "Sessions" = "sessions")
  ),

  checkboxInput("smooth", label = "Add smoother?",
    value = FALSE)
  )
),
```

The following are two more columns, each of width 3, making up the next two quarters of the row:

```
textOutput("textDisplay"),
plotOutput("trend")
  )
)
```

Finally, the full width of the screen is given over to the two outputs: the textual output that describes the numbers of days/users and the trend graph. Theoretically, these outputs could have been put within the `fluidRow(column(12, output))` instructions because the width of the screen is a fluid row containing one column of width 12, but you would never actually write this, and so it isn't used here either.

Version two – grid layout (B)

The interface that we just produced demonstrates a lot of the key concepts in layout, but it's horribly ugly. Let's produce a nice interface. Here's the finished product:

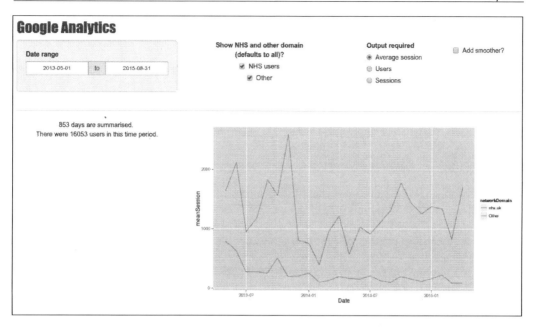

ui.R

Now we'll step through the `ui.R` file looking at all the changes made over the original version. The custom header is made as follows:

```
library(shiny)
shinyUI(fluidPage(
  title = "Google Analytics",
  h2("Google Analytics",
    style = "font-family: 'Impact';
    color: purple; font-size: 32px;"),
```

As we saw elsewhere, it's very easy to make your own headers using `h1()`, `h2()`, and so on and to pass style information into them as done in the preceding code. In this case, you can see also that we have passed `title = "Google Analytics"` to `fluidPage()` in order to give the window/tab a title on the web browser (equivalent to the HTML `<title>` tag).

The next chunk, the first `fluidRow()` layout with the input widgets, contains a few important changes:

```
fluidRow(
  column(4,
    wellPanel(
      dateRangeInput(inputId = "dateRange",
        label = "Date range",
        start = "2013-05-01")
    )
  ),
  column(4, div(
    checkboxGroupInput(inputId = "domainShow",
      label = HTML("Show NHS and other domain<br>
        (defaults to all)?"),
      choices = list("NHS users" = "nhs.uk",
        "Other" = "Other"),
      selected = c("nhs.uk", "Other")
    ),
    style = "text-align: center;"
  )
),
```

This section is set up with two columns, and both occupy one-third of the screen (`width = 4`). The date range widget in the first column has been placed within a well panel using the `wellPanel()` function to unobtrusively highlight it as an input widget. The second column has been placed within a `<div>` tag using the `div()` function with style information passed in (`style = "text-align: center;"`).

In order to break across the lines within the widget I have added `<br>` to the label, note that you will need to use HTML to wrap the string as the one in the preceding code to ensure that HTML is not escaped:

```
column(4,
  fluidRow(
    column(6,
      radioButtons(inputId = "outputRequired",
        label = "Output required",
        choices = list("Average session" =
          "meanSession",
          "Users" = "users",
          "Sessions" = "sessions")
      )
    ),
```

```
      column(6,
        checkboxInput("smooth", label = "Add smoother?",
          value = FALSE)
        )
      )
    )
  ), # end of fluidRow()
```

The preceding code chunk demonstrates nesting within grid layouts. In order to nest, simply add another fluid row within a column and subdivide up that column using the `column()` function (here you can note that each subcolumn occupies half that allocated space, using `width = 6`.)

The output part of the application demonstrates some of these same points, using `div()` and custom HTML tags to more finely control the appearance:

```
hr(),
fluidRow(
  column(4, div(
    htmlOutput("textDisplay"),
    style = "text-align: center;")
  ),
  column(8, plotOutput('trend'))
)
```

As you can see, `div()` is again used in order to allow custom styles to be passed in. The output of `output$textDisplay` is given by `htmlOutput()`, not `textOutput()`, because the text sent from `server.R` contains raw HTML, which we do not want to be escaped. The relevant chunk from `server.R` is shown as follows:

```
output$textDisplay <- renderText({
  paste(
    length(seq.Date(input$dateRange[1],
      input$dateRange[2], by = "days")),
      "days are summarised. <br>There were",
      sum(passData()$users),
      "users in this time period."
  )
})
```

As you can see, a `<br>` tag has been included in order to break the line at this point. Other than this change, the `server.R` file is the same as before.

Version three – navigation bar

Larger, more complex applications can be organized using a navigation bar along the top of the screen. The application we will look at is relatively simple to avoid generating too much code, but hopefully by the end of this section, you will be able to easily see how simple it is to organize a lot of UI elements in this way. The finished application is as follows:

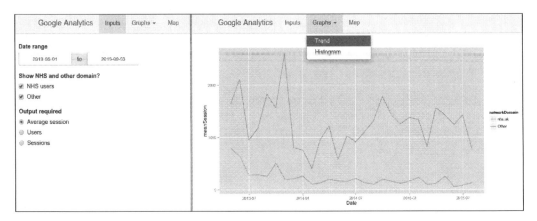

Two states of the application are shown; the inputs are shown on the first tab, and the graphs are stored in a menu in the second tab (menu pictured), and the map is shown on the final tab.

The `server.R` file is again unchanged except that the map drawing function that we saw in *Chapter 2, Building Your First Application*, has been put back in.

ui.R

Let's again look at the `ui.R` file:

```
shinyUI(
  navbarPage("Google Analytics",
```

The page is set up by using `navbarPage()` instead of `fluidPage()` and a title for the application passed in:

```
    tabPanel("Inputs",
      dateRangeInput(inputId = "dateRange",
        label = "Date range",
        start = "2013-05-01"),
      checkboxGroupInput(
        inputId = "domainShow",
```

```
      label = "Show NHS and other domain?",
      choices = list("NHS users" = "nhs.uk",
        "Other" = "Other"),
      selected = c("nhs.uk", "Other")
    ),
    radioButtons(inputId = "outputRequired",
      label = "Output required",
      choices = list("Average session" = "meanSession",
      "Users" = "users", "Sessions" = "sessions")
    )
  ),
```

Each tab panel gets a title (in this case, `Inputs`) and then a list of whichever input or output elements you wish, in this case, the date, domain select, and required output widgets. Look at the following code:

```
navbarMenu("Graphs",
  tabPanel("Trend", plotOutput("trend")),
  tabPanel("Histogram", plotOutput("histogram"))
),
```

Nesting elements within a submenu is achieved as mentioned earlier using the `navbarMenu()` function, with tab panels given within.

```
  tabPanel("Map", plotOutput("ggplotMap"))
)
)
```

We finish with the final tab panel, that is, the map function.

Version four – dashboard

This will be the most full-featured application in the chapter and has the longest `server.R` file. There are two changes to the server-side code for this version. The first is that we will add back in the code that reports on the client state using the `session$clientData` object.

This is featured in the first version of the application at the beginning of the chapter, and for convenience, it is featured again as follows:

```
shinyServer(function(input, output, session){
  [... other functions...]

  # (from http://shiny.rstudio.com/articles/client-data.html)
  cdata <- session$clientData
```

```
# Values from cdata returned as text
output$clientdataText <- renderText({
  cnames <- names(cdata)
  allvalues <- lapply(cnames, function(name) {
    paste(name, cdata[[name]], sep=" = ")
  })
  paste(allvalues, collapse = "\n")
})
[... ...]
})
```

Just for fun, we're also going to add in another map, using the leaflet package, which is available on CRAN-install with `install.packages("leaflet")`. This allows access to the functionality of the leaflet JavaScript library. For more details, visit the following URLs:

- `rstudio.github.io/leaflet/`
- `leafletjs.com/`

The code to produce the plot is as follows:

```
output$leaflet <- renderLeaflet({
  leaflet(gadf) %>% addCircles() %>% addTiles() %>%
  setView(lng = 1.1333, lat = 52.95, zoom = 4)
})
```

The leaflet package, and the JavaScript library on which it is based, offers a lot of functionality. This is a relatively simple instruction. The `leaflet()` function takes a dataframe and will automatically look for variables named `latitude` and `longitude`. Instructions are added to the leaflet call using the `%>%` operator from the magrittr package (`cran.r-project.org/web/packages/magrittr/`).

This will be familiar from its use in dplyr in *Chapter 2, Building Your First Application*. The `addCircles()` function plots each datapoint (that is, each IP address from which a request originated) and the `addTiles()` function plots the default map (many variations are possible, see the documentation for more). The `setView()` instruction tells the map the beginning location and zoom level. In this case, I have put in the latitude and longitude for Nottingham in the UK, which is where both I and the Trust for which I work are based, with a zoom level of four.

As you can see from the following picture, this level of zoom is appropriate for most of Europe. Just experiment with your own applications to get the right level of zoom (you could even pass the zoom level in using a shiny widget during testing, so you can experiment quickly yourself):

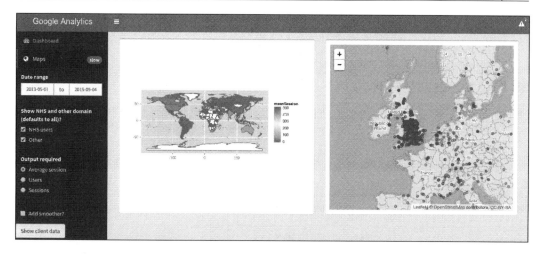

The main user interface looks as the following screenshot:

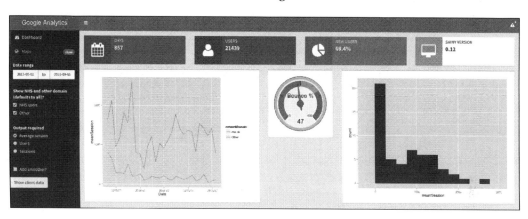

Ideally, go and download the application code available at chrisbeeley.net/website/ and run it on your machine or visit a hosted version of the application at goo.gl/Gft2V9. There is quite a bit of new functionality in this application, so it's a good idea to explore it now.

In case you can't do this, there follows a brief outline of the new functionality in the application:

- Notifications in the top-right of the interface
- Large friendly icons (info boxes) for key figures with icons (calendar, person, pie chart, Shiny version, and so on)
- Gauge in middle of screen with another key statistic (bounce rate)

We'll start by looking at the code for each of these additions and then move on to looking at how the whole UI is put together using the `shinydashboard` package.

Notifications

The ability to create notifications is part of a larger amount of functionality within shinydashboard, which allows you to create messages, tasks, and notifications in the header of your dashboard. For more details, visit `rstudio.github.io/shinydashboard/structure.html`.

In this example, we will just add notifications. The code is very similar to the other two types of content. On the `server.R` side, the code is as follows:

```
output$notifications <- renderMenu({
```

This line allows the notification content to be rendered dynamically and called in the `ui.R` file with `dropdownMenuOutput("notifications")`. We have the following code:

```
users <- sum(gadf[gadf$date == max(gadf$date), "users"])
newusers <- sum(gadf[gadf$date == max(gadf$date), "newUsers"]) /
sum(gadf[gadf$date == max(gadf$date), "users"])
* 100
```

These lines calculate the two values that we want— the number of users in the time period and the percentage of new users. We have the following code:

```
newusers <- round(newusers, 0)
notifData <- data.frame("number" = c(users, newusers),
  "text" = c(" users today",
    "% new users"),
  "icon"= c("users", "user")
)
```

Both values need to be stored in a data frame, which will force them to be of the same type. The value for new users is therefore rounded to an integer to avoid ugly decimals in both. In a production application, you might like to take a little more time to set up the interface so that you have the level of precision that you want by setting up each as a string, properly formatted as you desire.

We have avoided this here for brevity; for assistance with this task, you may wish to look at the help files for `format()`, `formatC()`, and `sprintf()`. The final dataframe looks like this:

```
> notifData
   number           text  icon
1       3  users today  users
2      67  % new users  user
>
```

Static notifications can be produced with the notificationItem() function as follows (with optional status and color arguments not used here):

```
notificationItem(
   text = "3 users today",
   icon("users")
   )
```

In order to produce content dynamically, we will make use of a function to produce a list of several notification items at once. This is achieved as follows:

```
notifs <- apply(notifData, 1, function(row) {
   notificationItem(text = paste0(row[["number"]],
     row[["text"]]),
   con = icon(row[["icon"]])
   )
})
```

As you can see, the data frame that we produced in the preceding code is processed row-wise with the appropriate values for text and icon being produced (text = "3 users today", icon = "users", and text = "67% new users", icon = "user").

```
dropdownMenu(type = "notifications", .list = notifs)
})
```

Finally, the menu is assembled using the dropdownMenu() function, which needs to pass the type (notifications, in this case) and either several notification items produced manually, as we saw in the preceding code, or as in this case, with the .list argument, a list of notification items, which will have usually been produced programmatically.

Having done all this, the actual notifications are passed into the header in the ui.R file quite simply like this:

```
header <- dashboardHeader(title = "Google Analytics",
   dropdownMenuOutput("notifications"))
```

This looks a little different to the usual structure that we have encountered, which is because unlike standard shiny interfaces, shiny dashboards are constructed from three separate sections—`dashboardHeader()`, `dashboardSidebar()`, and `dashboardBody()`. We will look in detail at the construction of a Shiny dashboard in the section on `ui.R` later.

Info boxes

We have already seen how to use icons earlier in the chapter, but Shiny dashboard makes a nice feature of it by expanding and coloring them to draw attention to key pieces of information. An info box can be drawn statically as follows:

```
infoBox(width = 3, "Shiny version", "0.12",
  icon = icon("desktop"))
```

As you can see, the width can be set (using the 12 span rule from the standard bootstrap functions we saw earlier in the chapter) with title (`Shiny version`) and value (`0.12`, although you may often wish to pass a number). This function is placed within `dashboardBody()` in the `ui.R` file.

Although you may sometimes wish to hard-code info boxes in this way (to show version numbers of an application, as in this case), in the majority of cases, you are going to produce this content dynamically. In this case, you will as always need to do some preparation on `server.R` first. Here is the code for the first info box:

```
output$days <- renderInfoBox({
  infoBox(
    "Days", input$dateRange[2] - input$dateRange[1],
    icon = icon("calendar", lib = "font-awesome"),
    color = "blue",
    fill = ifelse(max(passData()$date) == max(gadf$date),
      TRUE, FALSE)
  )
})
```

The first icon is the number of days within the specified range. The first argument gives the icon a title, (`Days`), the second gives it a value (the number of days, calculated by subtracting the first date from the second). You can also select the color of the box and whether the right-hand portion (which contains the text, as opposed to the icon) is filled (a solid color) or not.

As you can see, here we are deciding the fill of the value portion of the icon dynamically. When the user-selected range includes `today`, the icon will be filled. When it does not, it won't. See `?ifelse` for help with `ifelse()`.

The other dynamic info boxes are set up in the same way, as follows:

```
output$users <- renderInfoBox({
  infoBox(
    "Users", sum(passData()$users),
    icon = icon("user"),
    color = "purple",
    fill = ifelse(passData()$users /
      as.numeric(input$dateRange[2] -
        input$dateRange[1]) > 20,
    TRUE, FALSE)
  )
})

output$percentNew <- renderInfoBox({
  infoBox(
    "New users",
    paste0(round(sum(passData()$newUsers) /
      sum(passData()$users) * 100, 1), "%"),
    icon = icon("pie-chart"),
    color = "green",
    fill = ifelse(sum(passData()$newUsers) /
      sum(passData()$users) * 100 > 50,
      TRUE, FALSE)
  )
})
```

ui.R

The ui.R file to display the info boxes is similar to the function we already saw to display the static info box, except now the function is infoBoxOutput(). Putting all four info boxes together we now get:

```
fluidRow(
  infoBoxOutput(width = 3, "days"),
  infoBoxOutput(width = 3, "users"),
  infoBoxOutput(width = 3, "percentNew"),
  infoBox(width = 3, "Shiny version", "0.12",
    icon = icon("desktop"))
)
```

As elsewhere, in each case, infoBoxOutput() is given a string (days), which refers to the name of the corresponding output element (output$days).

Google Charts gauge

The gauge in the middle of the screen with the bounce rate is from the excellent Google Charts API. More information on this can be found at developers.google. com/chart/. Fortunately for us, there is an R package to interface with Google Charts, so there is no need to get our hands dirty with a different API. The package is on CRAN and can be installed with install.packages("googleVis").

The code is as follows:

```
output$gauge <- renderGvis({
  df <- data.frame(Label = "Bounce %",
    Value = round(mean(passData()$bounceRate,
      trim = .1), 1)
  )
  gvisGauge(df,
    options = list(min = 0, max = 100,
      greenFrom = 0,
      greenTo = 50, yellowFrom = 50,
      yellowTo = 70,
      redFrom = 70, redTo = 100)
  )
})
```

A data frame is produced, with the first column being the label for the gauge, and the second, the value of the gauge. If you require more than one gauge, simply include multiple rows. In this case, we will just use one row. The gauge is drawn very simply by passing the dataframe and a list of options, which are fairly self-explanatory, giving the minimum and maximum for the gauge as well as the limits where the gauge is green, yellow, and red, if desired. The gauge is drawn very simply on ui.R using htmlOutput("gauge").

Resizing the google chart

So far, it was so simple. However, there is a problem!

Google vis charts, unlike native R visualizations, are not automatically resized when the browser window changes. We're going to fix this problem very simply using session$clientData, which we came across at the beginning of the chapter. If you are running the application, click on the **Show client data** button at the bottom of the application. The following screen will appear:

Client Data ⊗

```
allowDataUriScheme = TRUE
output_clientdataText_hidden = FALSE
output_days_hidden = FALSE
output_gauge_hidden = FALSE
output_ggplotMap_hidden = TRUE
output_histogram_height = 400
output_histogram_hidden = FALSE
output_histogram_width = 554
output_leaflet_hidden = TRUE
output_notifications_hidden = FALSE
output_percentNew_hidden = FALSE
output_trend_height = 400
output_trend_hidden = FALSE
output_trend_width = 554
output_users_hidden = FALSE
pixelratio = 1
singletons =
url_hash_initial =
url_hostname = 127.0.0.1
url_pathname = /
url_port = 6039
url_protocol = http:
url_search =
```

Close

In order to redraw the gauge, we are going to establish a dependency on one of these elements that we know will change when the size of the browser window changes. In this case, `output_trend_width` is perfect. We're not really worried about height because there isn't anything to bump against the gauge below it, only to the left and right. The code to draw the gauge therefore becomes:

```
output$gauge <- renderGvis({
  # dependence on size of plots to detect a resize
  session$clientData$output_trend_width
  [... as before ...]
})
```

Changing the width of the browser window will now redraw the gauge, which will make it the right size again.

ui.R

Having examined all the new elements, we can have a look at how shiny dashboards are put together. As was briefly mentioned previously, Shiny dashboards are composed of three pieces—`dashboardHeader()`, `dashboardSidebar()`, and `dashboardBody()`. They can be put together like this:

```
dashboardPage(
   dashboardHeader([...]),
   dashboardSidebar([...]),
   dashboardBody([...])
)
```

Or they can be put together like this:

```
# produce components
header <- dashboardHeader([...])
sidebar <- dashboardSidebar([...])
body <- dashboardBody([...])

# assemble
dashboardPage(header, sidebar, body)
```

 I can't imagine ever using the former construction when the latter makes the code so much more readable, but to produce minimal and toy examples, you may prefer it.

We already saw the header part of the application previously; this is reproduced following for convenience. Note also that unlike in many Shiny applications, it is necessary to load several packages in the `ui.R` file because there are special functions within those packages, which get called with the file (for example. `dashboardHeader()`, `bsModal()`, `leafletOutput()`, and others). The top of the `ui.R` file therefore looks as follows:

```
library(shiny)
library(shinydashboard)
library(shinyBS)
library(leaflet)

header <- dashboardHeader(title = "Google Analytics",
   dropdownMenuOutput("notifications"))
```

The sidebar can contain input widgets, as is typical in Shiny applications, but also buttons to select different tabs of the dashboard, each of which can be set up to have different outputs on it. In this case, we have two tabs—the main one contains the graphs and icons we have spent most of this section discussing and a map tab contains the choropleth map, which featured in early versions of this application, as well as the interactive leaflet map.

The code is as follows:

```
sidebar <- dashboardSidebar(
  sidebarMenu(
    menuItem("Dashboard", tabName = "dashboard",
      icon = icon("dashboard")),
    menuItem("Maps", icon = icon("globe"), tabName = "map",
      badgeLabel = "slow", badgeColor = "red"),
```

The first two items are tab buttons that will allow us to present different sets of outputs to users. Each is given a title (Dashboard and Maps), a name (dashboard and maps), and an icon (dashboard and globe). The second item warns users that the map plotting functions are slow using the badgeLabel and badgeColor arguments, giving a red "slow" in this case.

The rest of the sidebar set up is familiar from previous incarnations of this application as follows:

```
    dateRangeInput(inputId = "dateRange", label = "Date range",
      start = "2013-05-01"), # select date
    checkboxGroupInput(inputId = "domainShow",
      label = HTML("Show NHS and other domain<br>
        (defaults to all)?"),
      choices = list("NHS users" = "nhs.uk",
        "Other" = "Other"),
      selected = c("nhs.uk", "Other")
    ),
    radioButtons(inputId = "outputRequired",
      label = "Output required",
      choices = list("Average session" = "meanSession",
        "Users" = "users",
        "Sessions" = "sessions")
    ),
    checkboxInput("smooth", label = "Add smoother?",
      value = FALSE),
    actionButton("showData", "Show client data")
  )
)
```

Finally, dashboardBody is set up using a tabItems(tabItem(), tabItem()) structure. Note that the bsModal() function is included here, to produce the pop-up. Including it with a tab item would result in its not working when the other tab was selected:

```
body <- dashboardBody(
  bsModal(id = "clientData", title = "Client Data",
    trigger = "showData",
    verbatimTextOutput("clientdataText")
  ),
  tabItems(
```

Each tab item will be passed into here; in this case, we have two, as we saw in the previous code—dashboard and maps.

```
    tabItem(tabName = "dashboard",
```

The tab item is given a name, which is the one we already used in the sidebar—dashboard.

```
      fluidRow(
        infoBoxOutput(width = 3, "days"),
        infoBoxOutput(width = 3, "users"),
        infoBoxOutput(width = 3, "percentNew"),
        infoBox(width = 3, "Shiny version", "0.12",
          icon = icon("desktop"))
      ),
```

Now you can put anything you like in it. In this case, we have a fluid row with four info boxes of width 3 (total width being 12, of course). The first three are the dynamic info boxes that we set up in the server.R file, and the third is a static version. The code for the static version, too, is featured earlier in this section.

```
      fluidRow(
        box(width = 5, plotOutput("trend")),
        box(width = 2, htmlOutput("gauge")),
        box(width = 5, plotOutput("histogram"))
      )
    ),
```

We finish the tab item with another fluid row. Note the use of the box() function that draws white boxes around the elements of a dashboard (see illustration of the interface earlier in the section).

```
tabItem(tabName = "map",
  box(width = 6, plotOutput("ggplotMap")),
  box(width = 6, leafletOutput("leaflet"))
  )
))
```

We finish with the final tab, map, which, as can be seen, consists of just two boxes containing the two maps that we drew in the server.R file.

Summary

In this chapter, we explored many different ways of laying out the same applications. Starting with the standard sidebar layout, we looked at adding icons, pop-ups, tooltips, and also using the shinythemes package to quickly style a vanilla application. We covered adding a navigation bar to your application as well as using the grid layout from bootstrap CSS to customize your own layouts. Finally, we explored the functionality of the Shiny dashboard package, which allows you to produce tabbed output sections, add in tasks, notifications, and messages for your users, show large friendly icons with key information on, as well as providing an attractive and professional-looking default appearance.

The key to make the most of the material in this chapter, as well as of Shiny generally, is to remember that you can combine the tools that Shiny gives you in a lot of different ways, depending on your needs and your skill set. There's nothing to stop you from using the shiny dashboard package with some highly customized HTML in one of the tabs if you need to very precisely build a particular kind of interface. Some developers who have more experience with JavaScript than with R may prefer to work with the Google Charts API in JavaScript and use Shiny as just a data workhorse, serving data or statistics straight to the JavaScript function. Think about what you need, and there will usually be a couple of ways to achieve it. The solution you pick will be based partly on producing an application that is simple, clean, and easy to maintain and debug.

In the next chapter, we are going to cover taking Shiny even further outside of the world of R using JavaScript, D3, and other visualization libraries, which can very simply be incorporated into your applications.

6
Advanced Applications II – Using JavaScript Libraries in Shiny Applications

In this chapter, we're going to take a look at user-contributed packages, which allow you to easily use JavaScript plotting libraries in your Shiny applications. It is, of course, possible to use JavaScript and its libraries in Shiny by writing all the code yourself, and we covered incorporating JavaScript in an application in *Chapter 3, Building Your Own Web Pages with Shiny*. You may need to write something very specific in JavaScript, but if you wish to use some of the wonderful graphical libraries in JavaScript, you may find that somebody has done all of the hard work for you and produced an R package, which allows you to produce the graphics straight from R. In this chapter, we will take a look at some of the user-contributed packages, which allow you to access JavaScript plotting straight from R, and some of the plots, which they enable you to produce. However, there are other examples out there and this is just designed to give you a flavor of what's possible. There are loads of more examples at http://www.htmlwidgets.org/. In this chapter, we will cover the following topics:

- Learning how to use and extend htmlwidgets, the Shiny package that makes all this possible
- Drawing trend and prediction data using the dygraphs package
- Using NVD3 and rCharts to produce highly interactive and easy-to-use plots
- Drawing a heatmap with d3heatmap and learning about JavaScript library conflicts and resolving them in Shiny
- Producing an interactive 3D map of the world and plotting Google Analytics to use data on it using threejs

The htmlwidgets package

The `htmlwidgets` package is the magic sauce that makes all of the packages in this chapter work. Essentially, it allows package developers to very easily produce bindings between JavaScript visualization libraries and R. If you wish to make use of the `htmlwidgets` package to produce a binding to your own favorite JavaScript library, then it is a relatively simple process, details of which can be found at `http://www.htmlwidgets.org/develop_intro.html`. We will not look at the process of producing your own bindings because many popular libraries are available, and there are plenty in this chapter that demonstrate the use of existing libraries. Moreover, it requires competence with JavaScript, which is not assumed in this book. We can say that the `htmlwidgets` package makes it easy to use JavaScript visualization libraries from R, including R Markdown documents and Shiny applications.

In this chapter, we will build a large, multi-tabbed Shiny application to show off some of the things that `htmlwidgets` and the package authors, who have used `htmlwidgets`, have made easy. Each section of the following and each tab will contain a visualization from a different package.

The application framework

Most of the code in this chapter expands on the Google Analytics application, as described in *Chapter 2, Building Your First Application*. Before we begin, let's review the code in `server.R`, which sets the data ready for the plotting commands. The complete code can be downloaded and run from `http://chrisbeeley.net/website/`:

```
library(dplyr)
library(shiny)
library(dygraphs)
library(xts)
library(rCharts)
library(d3heatmap)
```

Here, we load all of the packages, which will be needed for the application. The new ones can be installed as follows:

```
install.packages(c("dygraphs", "xts", "d3heatmap"))
require(devtools)
install_github("ramnathv/rCharts")
```

Now, we begin with the application, using the `session` argument. As described in *Chapter 4, Taking Control of Reactivity, Inputs, and Outputs*, this is necessary to allow us to customize the UI based on which tab is currently selected:

```
shinyServer(function(input, output, session) {
  load("gadf.Rdata")
  gadf$weekday = weekdays(gadf$date)
  gadf$yearmon = as.Date(
    paste0(substr(gadf$YearMonth, 1, 4), "-",
      substr(gadf$YearMonth, 5, 6), "-01")
  )
```

As mentioned earlier, the data is loaded in, but in this case, there are some extra commands that add the days of the week and change the `YearMonth` variable to a real date that is ready to be plotted using the `dygraphs` package. For more on the first command see `?weekdays`, the second command simply takes the year, the month, and `01` and pastes them all together with a - separating each, before converting to a date (for example, `201503` becomes `2015-03-01`). For more see `?substr`.

```
# reactive data
passData <- reactive({
  firstData <- filter(
    gadf, date >= input$dateRange[1] & date <=
    input$dateRange[2]
  )
  if(!is.null(input$domainShow)){
    firstData <- filter(
      firstData, networkDomain %in% input$domainShow
    )
  }
  return(firstData)
})
```

The data is produced as mentioned earlier, as summarized in the preceding code.

```
# control the checkboxes
observe({
  if(length(input$domainShow) == 0){
    updateCheckboxGroupInput(
      session, "domainShow",
```

```
        choices = list ("NHS users" = "nhs.uk",
          "Other" = "Other"),
        selected = c("nhs.uk", "Other")
      )
    }
  })
```

Finally, we take control of the domain selection checkboxes, as we did in
Chapter 4, Taking Control of Reactivity, Inputs, and Outputs, in order to prevent the
user from deselecting both and leaving us with no data. Let's now turn our attention
to the ui.R file that will give an indication of the inputs, which each part of the
application will accept.

ui.R

Because all of the tabs produce different kinds of outputs, we will make an extensive
use of the conditionalPanel() function (which, you will recall, shows, or hides UI
elements, depending on preset conditions) to ensure that users are not confused by
UI elements that either don't do anything or, even worse, break the application. Also,
note that it is necessary to load some of the packages that we will be using in the
preamble to the ui.R file as well because they have special functions to show their
outputs (such as dygraphOutput, globeOutput, and so on).

```
library (shiny)
library (dygraphs)
library (rCharts)
library (d3heatmap)
library (threejs)
shinyUI (fluidPage (
    # Application title
    titlePanel("Google Analytics"),
```

In the preceding code, we can see all of the requisite packages being loaded and a
simple UI setup defined.

```
sidebarLayout (
    sidebarPanel (
      dateRangeInput (inputId = "dateRange", label = "Date range",
        start = "2013-05-01"), # select date
```

The date range is common to all of the tabs and so this is the only input that will not be wrapped in `conditionalPanel()`. It is unchanged from the previous version of this application in *Chapter 2, Building Your First Application*.

```
conditionalPanel(
    condition = "input.theTabs != 'barchart' &
    input.theTabs != 'heatmap' & input.theTabs != 'globe'",
    checkboxGroupInput(inputId = "domainShow",
        label = "Show NHS and other domain
        (defaults to all)?",
        choices = list("NHS users" = "nhs.uk",
            "Other" = "Other"),
        selected = c("nhs.uk", "Other")
    ),
    hr()
),
```

In the preceding code, we can see a `conditionalPanel()` instruction incorporating a JavaScript test that decides whether to show the selector for the NHS and other domains. This is not shown when the currently selected tab is the `heatmap`, `barchart`, or `globe` output because each of these incorporates data from around the world and the NHS only exists in UK; therefore, allowing users to deselect the NHS would break the application. Make a note of the way in which the names of tabs are represented in JavaScript. In a Shiny application, as discussed in *Chapter 4, Taking Control of Reactivity, Inputs, and Outputs*, named tabs are represented by `input$nameOfTabPanel = "nameOfIndividualTab"`. This translates into JavaScript as `input.nameOfTabPanel = "nameOfIndividualTab"`. In this case, the tab panel has been called `theTabs` (as you will see in the rest of the UI definition mentioned later in and, for example, the **Heatmap** tab is called `heatmap`, making the JavaScript test `input.theTabs != "heatmap"`. Logical tests are linked together in many languages (including R, of course) using `&` for and.

Finally, `hr()` draws a horizontal line underneath the selector just to break the interface a bit:

```
conditionalPanel(
    condition = "input.theTabs != 'heatmap'",
    radioButtons(inputId = "outputRequired",
        label = "Output required",
        choices = list(
            "Average session" = "meanSession",
            "Users" = "users", "Sessions" = "sessions"
        )
    )
),
```

The following code is another conditional panel statement; this one merely excludes the variable selector when the `heatmap` tab is selected. This is done because the `heatmap` tab automatically includes all the variables that are fed to it (as shown in the following code), so the variable selector would serve no purpose and confuse the user:

```
conditionalPanel(
   condition = "input.theTabs == 'trend'",
   sliderInput("roll", "Select roll period",
     min = 1, max = 10, value = 5)
   )
),
```

You may wish, instead, to disable the field rather than have it vanish completely. This is a little complex and involves using your own JavaScript or the `shinyjs` package, which includes a helper function for this operation. This is not covered in this book.

The final conditional panel includes a rolling smooth selector that only appears when the `dygraphs` trend plot is drawn; this is because only the `dygraphs` statement includes this functionality, and so including it elsewhere would confuse the user.

```
mainPanel(
   tabsetPanel(id = "theTabs",
```

Here, we set up the output panel, as you can see that the tabset panel is given the name `theTabs` (this was referenced earlier in the JavaScript test for `conditionalPanel`):

```
tabPanel("Trend", dygraphOutput("trend"),
   br(), hr(),
   textOutput("textDisplay"),
   value = "trend"
   ),
```

The first tab is given the name `trend` and includes two outputs: a graph from the `dygraphs` package (based on the `dygraphs` JavaScript library: http://dygraphs.com/), which we will look at shortly and a textual summary of the number of days that the output summarizes. Make a note of the use of `dygraphOutput()` instead of `plotOutput()`.

```
tabPanel("Prediction",
   dygraphOutput("predictSeries"),
   br(), hr(),
```

```
p("Predict function based on code",
  a(href = "http://rstudio.github.io/dygraphs/
    gallery-upper-lower-bars.html", "here"),
  value = "prediction")
),
```

The second tab is named `prediction` and it includes another `dygraphs` output as well as some static text, indicating the source of the code in the `Predict` function. Make a note of the use of the `a()` function that produces an HTML link from two arguments: the first to give the URL and the second the text, which is readable to the user. Again, note the use of `dygraphOutput()`.

```
tabPanel("Barchart",
  showOutput("barchart", lib =  "nvd3"),
  hr(),
  p("Note that number of sessions and users uses a log
    scale"),
  value = "barchart"
),
```

The third tab is named `barchart` and makes use of the rCharts (`http://rcharts.io/`) package and the NVD3 (`http://nvd3.org/`) JavaScript (that is, D3) library. Note the use of `showOutput()` as well as the `lib` argument that tells Shiny which JavaScript library the plot is based on. Make a note of the name passed to `showOutput()` and `barchart`; this forms part of the DOM of the page, and we will manually add the plot to this area in the `server.R` file code that produces the rCharts output.

Using the `p()` function, a note is added to inform users that the number of sessions and users is plotted on a log scale.

```
tabPanel("Heatmap",
  uiOutput("ui_heatmap"),
  value = "heatmap"
),
```

The fourth tab is named `heatmap`, and it includes a `heatmap` from the `d3heatmap` package (which is itself based on vanilla D3). In this case, we have taken the unusual step of using `uiOutput()`, which, if you remember, is the function that produces dynamic UI components server-side (defined in `server.R`). This is not typical within the `d3heatmap` package; however, in this case, the use of two different JavaScript libraries on the same page (NVD3 from the rCharts example mentioned earlier and vanilla D3 from this package) produces a conflict, and Shiny fails to render the `heatmap` correctly. Rendering the UI dynamically on this page ensures that the UI is redrawn when it is selected, which enables the correct JavaScript library and makes the plot work. We will see the UI definition later in this chapter when we take a look at the `server.R` file in detail.

```
tabPanel("Globe",
  globeOutput("globe"), value = "globe")
)
```

The last tab is called `globe`, and it includes the output from the `threejs` package that is based on the `threejs` JavaScript library (`http://threejs.org/`), which is designed to produce plots and graphics in 3D. The R implementation includes two main kinds of output: 3D scatterplots and plots on globes (including Earth and other planets and celestial bodies, if you wish). Note the use of `globeOutput()` in place of `plotOutput()`:

```
    )
  )
))
```

That's it for the UI; it's pretty simple once the conditional panels are set up, and the tabset and panels are each given a name. Having set up the UI, we are now ready to define the plotting functions, so let's first turn our attention to a simple time series graph using the `dygraphs` package.

Dygraphs

The `dygraphs` library in JavaScript (`http://dygraphs.com/`) is designed to show the time series and trend data. It supports zoom, pan, mouseover, and even supports mobile devices by offering pinch to zoom. The `dygraphs` R package provides a handy interface to many of the functions of the `dygraphs` library. It can be installed using `install.packages("dygraphs")`.

We'll take a look at a few of the things that can be done with the package here. Let's take a look at the finished graph:

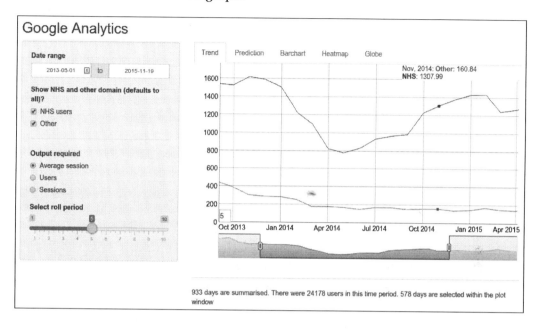

There are a couple of things you need to make a note of on this graph. Firstly, you can see the mouseover effect at the top-right of the graph, where the date and values of **NHS** and **Other** are listed. Secondly, this graph has been smoothed using a rolling average. The number of points to be averaged is specified in the widget on the left-hand side of the page (**Select roll period**) and is given by default in the small square box at the bottom-left of the graph. Thirdly, the grey box at the bottom with the selector on either side can be used to select date ranges on the graph. This can be useful in a Shiny application as a way of keeping the date range of all the data constants but allowing the user to zoom in on the graph as they choose. As you can see, the text underneath the graph makes this distinction clear, reporting the number of days in the whole dataset (933) as well as the number selected on the graph itself (578). Making a graph user friendly and interactive is extremely easy using the `dygraphs` package. Let's take a look at the portion of `server.R`, which makes it work.

server.R

Although the plotting function is very simple indeed (three lines in this case, as you can see at the end of this section), we need to set the data into a form that `dygraphs` will accept. Further, because this is a Shiny application, we need to accept different combinations of inputs. This next section is, therefore, a little bit longer than some other plotting functions that are elsewhere in the book. Considering the interactivity that `dygraphs` offers straight from the box, it's easy to see that it's definitely worth taking out some of your time getting it to work. We'll walk you through the whole plotting function and finish with a nice, simple, and clear plotting instruction:

```r
output$trend <- renderDygraph({
```

The first thing that we need to make a note of is that `dygraphs` are rendered with `renderDygraph({...})` and not `renderPlot({...})`.

```r
otherData <- filter(passData(), networkDomain == "Other") %>%
group_by(yearmon, networkDomain) %>%
summarise(meanSession = mean(sessionDuration, na.rm = TRUE),
  users = sum(users),
  sessions = sum(sessions)
)

nhsData <- filter(passData(), networkDomain == "nhs.uk") %>%
group_by(yearmon, networkDomain) %>%
summarise(meanSession = mean(sessionDuration, na.rm = TRUE),
  users = sum(users), sessions = sum(sessions)
)
```

This code is similar to the code that we have seen in the other chapters; here, we are producing two datasets: one for the NHS network domain and one for the other network domains. The `filter()` function from the `dplyr` package very easily allows us to select only data from the two respective domains, which is then passed as normal with `dplyr` with `>%>` to other functions, which group and summarize the data.

```r
otherSeries = xts(
  otherData[, input$outputRequired],
  order.by = otherData$yearmon
)
```

```
nhsSeries = xts(
  nhsData[, input$outputRequired],
  order.by = nhsData$yearmon
)
```

The next two instructions take the data that we just produced and place it in an `xts` (extensible time series) object. The `dygraphs` package is happy to accept `xts` objects, and remember that we loaded the `xts` library in the preamble to this application. The code is very simple; we extract the variable that we want using the `input$outputRequired` variable, which is passed from the UI, and specifies whether the user wants to see the mean session duration, the number of users, or the number of sessions. The `order.by` argument simply takes the `date` variable that we have set, as described previously. It must be unique, ordered, and a time-based class (for example, the `Date` class and the `POSIXct` class).

```
if(length(input$domainShow) > 1){
  toPlot = cbind(otherSeries, nhsSeries)
  names(toPlot) = c("Other", "NHS")
} else if(input$domainShow == "nhs.uk"){
  toPlot = nhsSeries
  names(toPlot) = c("NHS")
} else if(input$domainShow == "Other"){
  toPlot = otherSeries
  names(toPlot) = c("Other")
}
```

This section handles all of the different outputs that users can request: whether it's both NHS and other network domains, or just one. In both the cases, it's a simple case of using `cbind()` to combine them together; this can be plugged straight into the `dygraph()` function. In each case, the series is given appropriate names.

```
dygraph(toPlot) %>%
dyRangeSelector(height = 50) %>%
dyRoller(rollPeriod = input$roll)
})
```

Finally, as promised, we get a simple and clear plotting instruction. The first function draws the main plot and will suffice on its own, producing this result:

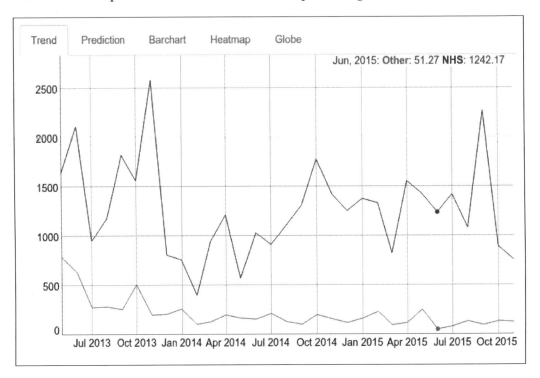

Using the `magrittr` pipe, we can pass this basic plot to the other two functions, which add extra functionalities. The `dyRangeSelector()` function adds to the gray box, which we saw at the bottom of the graph in the full application, allowing the user to zoom in and out on the graph. In this case, a `height` argument is passed (I felt that the default was a little small), but there are other options, such as color, default zoom level, and so on. As always, for more information, refer to `?dyRangeSelector`. Finally, the `dyRoller()` function provides smoothing by averaging over a given number of data points. In this case, you can see that we can use the value from the `input$roll` numeric slider to determine the number of points. Remember that we saw this being placed in a conditional panel, which only appears when this tab is selected in the main UI section at the beginning of this chapter.

Dygraphs with a prediction

Although we've already looked at dygraphs, it's worth looking at it again, so we can see how to build a prediction in the final plot. This is quite simple to do, and the particular prediction statistics that we will use here has few assumptions about the data and can be used in most contexts. Before we take a look at the code, let's take a look at the final application:

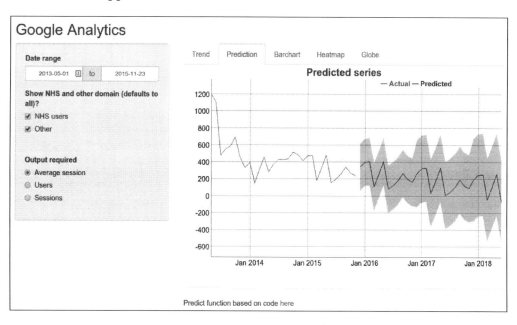

As you can see, the graph contains the actual data as well as a prediction of how the data might look over the next few years. The blue shading indicates prediction intervals, which give us an idea of the reliability of the projection. Let's now turn our attention to the code to produce this plot:

```
output$predictSeries <- renderDygraph({
```

Again, the graph is produced using the special renderDygraph() function.

```
theSeries <- group_by(passData(), yearmon) %>%
summarise(meanSession = mean(sessionDuration, na.rm = TRUE),
  users = sum(users), sessions = sum(sessions)
)
```

As mentioned earlier, we first produce the summarized data.

```
finalSeries = ts(
  theSeries[, input$outputRequired],
  start =
    c(as.numeric(substr(theSeries$yearmon[1], 1, 4)),
      as.numeric(substr(theSeries$yearmon[1], 6, 7))
    ),
  frequency = 12)

hw <- HoltWinters(finalSeries,
  gamma = length(finalSeries) > 24)
p <- predict(hw,
  n.ahead = length(finalSeries),
  prediction.interval = TRUE)
all <- cbind(finalSeries, p)
```

Secondly, we produce a normal time series object using `ts()`. Having done this, we produce a predicted series using the `HoltWinters()` and `predict()` functions (for more information, refer to `?HoltWinters`). The `gamma` argument checks whether seasonality should be applied to the model; this is only possible when two cycles of data exist (in this case, two cycles of 12 months gives 24 data points), and so `gamma` is `TRUE`, when there is enough data and `FALSE` when there is not enough data. The `predict()` function makes the actual predicted series used for plotting. In this case, `n.ahead` is given the value of the length of the series, so the prediction is always as long as the data and `prediction.interval` is `TRUE` so that prediction intervals can be drawn. The assumptions for Holt Winters prediction intervals are actually a little more stringent than for its uses without prediction intervals, but it produces a nice graphical effect if you use them. In your own applications, you will, of course, want to carefully check the assumptions of any statistical methods you employ. Finally, the original series and the predicted parts are joined using a simple `cbind()` instruction.

```
dygraph(all, "Predicted series") %>%
dySeries("finalSeries", label = "Actual") %>%
dySeries(c("p.lwr", "p.fit", "p.upr"), label = "Predicted")
})
```

As mentioned earlier, we finish with a beautiful, simple plotting instruction. Firstly, the collection of series (the original, prediction, and prediction intervals) is passed to the `dygraph()` command. This will draw all the data and produce a graph like this:

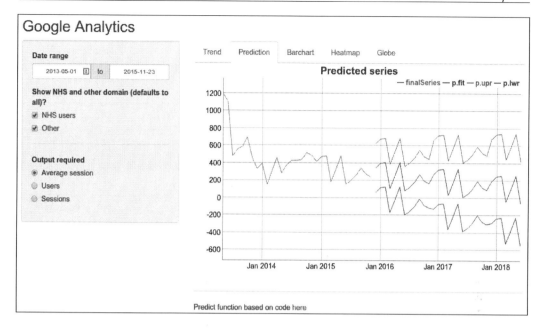

In the preceding graph, there are lines in the predicted series for the prediction itself as well as its lower and upper bounds. In order to tidy up the graph and produce shaded intervals, it is necessary to pipe this plotting instruction to two `dySeries()` commands, as shown in the preceding graph. The first instruction gives a label to the original data and the second specifies the prediction, lower and upper parts of the latter part of the series, which results in a nice shaded plot that we saw in the original image of this application. Refer to `?dySeries` for more information.

rCharts

The support within rCharts for different JavaScript libraries is very broad, and there are many possibilities of producing beautiful, interactive graphics. Here, we will take a look at just one and peruse the documentation at `http://rcharts.io/` to see the different libraries and graphs supported by the package.

The `rCharts` package is not available on CRAN but can be installed very easily using the following code:

```
install.packages("devtools")
require(devtools)
install_github("ramnathv/rCharts")
```

Let's now take a look at one of the many plot outputs possible with this package. The final application tab looks like this:

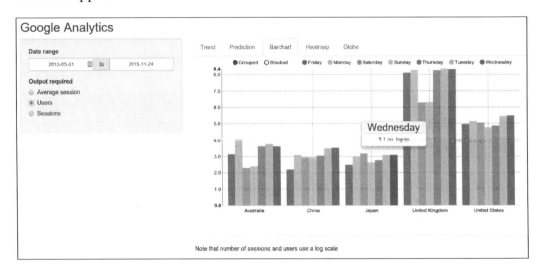

This plot is a clustered bar chart of the selected input (**Average session/Users/ Sessions**), showing the numbers on each day and in five different countries. Note that the number of sessions and users is logged because the UK has far more of these than any other country (as you would expect), and using a logged scale, makes the graph fit on the page better. Thanks to the magic of D3, the plot is interactive out of the box. It supports mouseover, as shown in the preceding screenshot, with Japan's results for **Wednesday** highlighted. The plot can be changed from **Grouped** to **Stacked** (that is, different days grouped horizontally or vertically), and the days of the week can be hidden and shown by clicking on them at the top in the legend of the graph. This wonderful graph can be produced with almost no code at all, as shown in the following code:

```
output$barchart <- renderChart({
  groupCountry <- group_by(passData()[passData()$country %in%
    c("United Kingdom", "United States",
      "Australia", "China", "Japan"), ],
    country, weekday) %>%
    summarise(meanSession = mean(sessionDuration),
      users = log(sum(users)),
      sessions = log(sum(sessions)
    )
  )
```

Most of the code is in this `dplyr` instruction that groups the data by a country and weekday (first, choose a dataset with only five countries). Note the use of `renderChart()` instead of `renderPlot()`.

```
thePlot <- nPlot(x = "country", y = input$outputRequired,
    data = groupCountry, group = "weekday",
    type = "multiBarChart")
```

Plotting can be done using a lattice-style formula interface (`SepalLength ~ SepalWidth | Species, data = iris`) or the base graphics-style `x = "SepalWidth", y = "SepalLength"`. In this case, we need to use the `x` and `y` style notation because `y` will be passed a string by Shiny (the contents of `input$outputRequired`).

```
thePlot$addParams(dom = 'barchart')
return(thePlot)
```

It is necessary to add the plot to the DOM using `thePlot$addParam`. We have already named `thePlot` in the `nplot` function, and the `dom` argument should match the component in the UI, which refers to the `rChart` (we covered the UI definition at the beginning of this chapter, and the relevant part is `showOutput("barchart", lib = "nvd3")`). Remember that we pass the type of library required to the `showOutput()` function in `ui.R`; in this case, the library is NVD3:

```
})
```

d3heatmap

The `d3heatmap` package uses vanilla D3 and produces interactive `heatmaps`. It can be installed using `install.packages("d3heatmap")`. The output looks like the following screenshot:

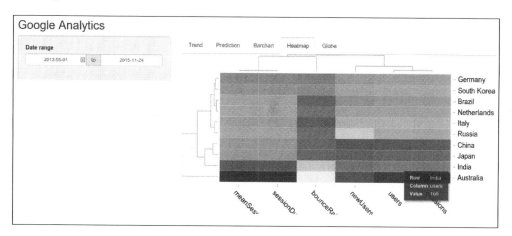

In the preceding screenshot, several variables are plotted (arranged along the *x* axis) for 10 countries (arranged along the *y* axis). Mouseover is supported, as shown in the preceding screenshot, with the result for users in India that is highlighted (108). The code is as follows:

```
output$ui_heatmap <- renderUI({
   d3heatmapOutput("heatmap")
})
```

The first thing to note that, as discussed at the beginning of this chapter, is that it is necessary to draw the UI in a reactive context. This is because the JavaScript functions from the rCharts (NVD3) output interfere with the JavaScript (D3) from this output. Providing a reactive context for the UI ensures that this output is redrawn and allows the plot to be displayed properly. This is quite simple, as we merely need to wrap the standard d3heatmap() output function (which would normally be placed in ui.R) in renderUI().

```
output$heatmap = renderD3heatmap({
```

Now, all that remains is the main plotting function, which you can see is placed in renderD3heatmap() as opposed to renderPlot().

```
toPlot = group_by(passData()[passData()$country !=
   "(not set)", ], country) %>%
summarise(meanSession = mean(sessionDuration, na.rm = TRUE),
   users = sum(users), newUsers = sum(newUsers),
   sessions = sum(sessions),
   sessionDuration = mean(sessionDuration),
   bounceRate = mean(bounceRate)
) %>%
arrange(desc(users))
```

In this application, we first use dplyr to produce a summary of the data to be plotted. In this case, we are calculating a few more variables than usual because heatmaps are good to summarize lots of variables. The arrange() function is used to rank the countries in a descending order of the numbers of users to produce a list headed by countries that have reasonably large amounts of user activity, so there is something to be plotted.

```
d3heatmap(toPlot[3:12, -1], scale = "column",
   labRow = toPlot[[1]][3:12], colors = "YlOrRd")
})
```

Having prepared the data, the actual plotting instruction itself is very simple. The data passed to the `toPlot[3:12, -1]` function removes the first column (which contains row names) and includes 10 countries, from the third heaviest user to the twelfth heaviest user. The first two (the UK and US) are excluded because they have many more users than the other countries, which makes the scale difficult to discern. The `scale` argument indicates that we wish to center and scale the values along with columns (as opposed to rows or neither). The `labRow` argument is given the row names from the first column of the data that `dplyr` returns. Finally, the color spectrum is selected; this argument takes several different types of values; in this case, a `http://colorbrewer2.org/` name, which gives yellows, oranges, and reds. For more information on specifying palettes or other ways of customizing outputs from `d3heatmap`, refer to `?d3heatmap`.

threejs

The `threejs` package, as discussed at the beginning of the chapter, can be used to produce 3D scatterplots or plots on globe mappings (including Earth and celestial bodies). It can be installed using `install.packages("threejs")`. In order to produce the globe output that is shown in this section, it is necessary to also install maps using `install.packages("maps")`. The finished application tab looks like this:

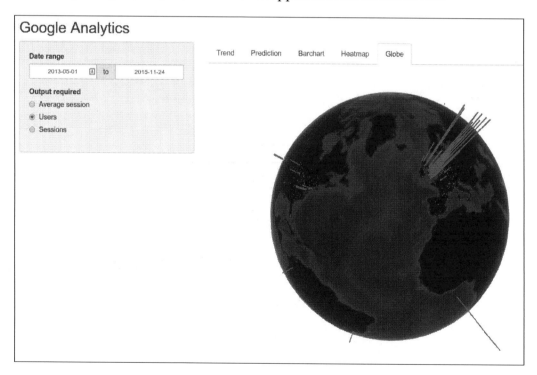

The code is as follows:

```
output$globe <- renderGlobe({
  if(input$outputRequired == "meanSession"){
    globejs(lat = passData()$latitude,
      long = passData()$longitude,
      value = mean(passData()$sessionDuration, na.rm = TRUE),
      bg = "white", color = "green", atmosphere = TRUE)
  } else {
```

This piece of code is executed when the user wishes to view the mean session values. As shown in the preceding code, the average of the sessionDuration variable is found.

```
    globejs(lat = passData()$latitude,
      long = passData()$longitude,
      value = log(passData()[, input$outputRequired]) * 50,
      bg = "white", color = "green", atmosphere = TRUE)
  }
})
```

If either of the other two variables is selected, then this is passed via input$outputRequired and logged, as mentioned earlier, because there is a large variation in the numbers of users and sessions, and using a logged scale, the figure becomes more readable. The actual plotting itself is very easy once the data is in the right format (which Google Analytics data will be, since it includes the latitude and longitude), and you only need to specify the latitude, longitude, and variable of interest in order to produce a beautiful, interactive globe. In this case, we have specified the color of the points (green) and turned on an atmosphere effect, which uses the WebGL graphics (hardware accelerated graphics for JavaScript).

Summary

In this chapter, we have used a lot of different JavaScript libraries and R packages and have produced a diverse range of plots, many of which you will find useful in your own applications. It's universally true that the actual plotting instructions themselves are very simple (although you can highly customize the output with different arguments) as long as your data is in the right format. It's worth taking the time to understand the types of inputs the packages accept, and if you don't get the results, you want a good place to start fixing the problem by looking at the structure of the input (run `str(theInput)` to have R show you the structure of an input). Another potential source of problems is to ensure that Shiny passes arguments to your functions in the correct way. Keep in mind that they will often be strings that will not always function in the same way as in standard R plotting instructions (for example, in the rCharts example, when using a formula-based plotting instruction). The debugging advice in *Chapter 4*, *Taking Control of Reactivity, Inputs, and Outputs*, will prove to be useful here, particularly, when using `cat(input$problemInput)` or `cat(str(input$problemInput))` to examine the content and structure of the variables, which Shiny passes to your plotting functions.

There are more packages using `htmlwidgets` and more plots that are available than the ones we looked at here. So, once you have explored the material in this chapter, read the documentation, go to `http://www.htmlwidgets.org/`, see what's out there, and have some fun incorporating it into your own applications.

7
Sharing Your Creations

Having made all of these wonderfully intuitive and powerful applications, you are quite naturally going to want to show them off. You may wish to share them with colleagues or members of the worldwide R community. You may wish to share them with individuals in your department or field who, while not R users, can handle a little bit of effort to get an application working. Or you may wish to share them transparently and freely with the whole world by hosting them on a server.

Shiny offers quite a lot of approaches to sharing applications, and you'll be glad to hear that even the most complex should not be too taxing with the right hardware and OS on your server. In this chapter, we will take a look at the following:

- Sharing your work with R users using Gist or GitHub
- Using .zip and .tar files locally or over the Internet to share an application
- Sharing over the Web using free and paid-for hosting and technologies from Rstudio
- Reusing data across Shiny applications hosted on a server
- Browser compatibility within Shiny

Sharing with the R community

Sharing with the R community is a little easier than with a general audience for two reasons:

- They can run the Shiny package within R and, therefore, use the Shiny functions designed to help distribute Shiny packages
- They are almost guaranteed to be reasonably knowledgeable about some of the processes that help you distribute an application, for example, unzipping directories

There are a few ways of sharing with R users running the Shiny package within R summarized in the following sections.

Sharing over GitHub

By far, the easiest way of sharing your creations with fellow R users is over GitHub (github.com). Of course, other R users can also use all the other methods in this chapter, but this is probably the most frictionless method (short of hosting the application) for both you and the end user.

An introduction to Git

You will no doubt have heard of Git (git-scm.com—the version control system that has collaborative sharing features at GitHub) even if you have never used it. Git is a version control system that can be used locally on your computer, or in order to get the best out of it, the version control repository on your computer can be synced online at GitHub. Hosting of open source code at GitHub is free, and there are paid options for closed source code.

If you haven't already used a version control, this is an excellent reason to start it. It is a little intimidating for newcomers, but over time, the resources and tutorials on the site have improved and perhaps one day of head scratching awaits you. Trust me that one day I will be paid back hundredfold. The Pro Git book can be downloaded for free from the Git site at git-scm.com/book/en/v2. There is also a wonderful interactive tutorial (try.github.io) on the Git site.

As a die-hard Linux enthusiast, it pains me to admit it, but I actually found learning on Windows easier because they provide a wonderful GUI to get you started (also on OS X). This does not mean that you need to use Windows or should stick to Windows; I happily dropped the GUI and went to the terminal in Linux once I'd found my feet a bit.

> It's also worth noting that there are some great GUIs for Linux as well, so you can check your package management system. I didn't find any that supported beginners so well as the official Windows or OS X versions, though. Git has a list of GUIs at git-scm.com/downloads/guis. Note that some of these support GitHub and others support Git itself. The list includes Windows, OS X, and Linux GUIs.

Finally, RStudio itself actually supports Git and GitHub, and once you've installed Git and set up your account, you can pretty much run the whole show from within RStudio itself.

Using Git and GitHub within Rstudio

To install Git, simply go to the URL mentioned earlier and download the `.exe` file for Windows, or on Ubuntu, run the following command:

```
sudo apt-get install git
```

For other flavors of Linux, check the package management system. Having installed Git, you now need to set up a new project within RStudio. A version control with Git (or SVN, a different version control system, which we will not consider here) is only possible when we use a project within RStudio.

Projects in RStudio

Using projects in RStudio is a way to organize your work. Each project has its own working directory with a separate R session, workspace, console input history, and open editor tabs (among other things). Each time a project is opened, each of these will be set to the value currently associated with the project, in effect launching a new R session, loading the data and console history since the last time the project was used (if they are selected as the default behavior or individually for this project), setting the working directory to the one associated with the project, and so on. This allows you to switch in and out of different projects either as you work or when you pick up work the next day.

To set up a new project, go to **File | New Project** in RStudio. The following menu will appear:

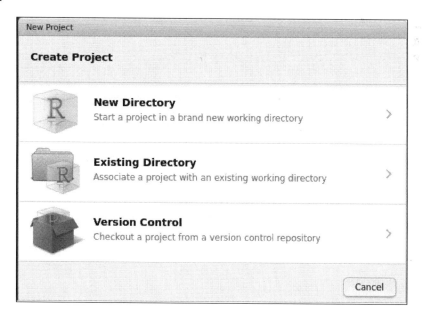

Select either **New Directory** if this is a completely new set of code and files that you want to create a new folder for or **Existing directory** if you have already started and just want to point the project to a directory, which you have already created.

Once you have a project set up, go to **Tools | Version control | Project setup**. The following menu will appear:

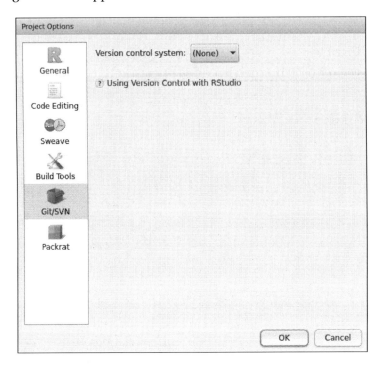

Make sure that the **Git/SVN** tab on the left-hand side of the page is selected and use the version control system control on the right-hand side of the page to select **Git/SVN**, if you prefer, but this will only appear if you have installed it, and this will not be covered in this chapter). You may need to reopen the project at this point by going to **File | Recent projects**.

You will need to configure the remote connection between your local .git repository and the GitHub account yourself. Go to your GitHub account, and go to **Repositories | New**. Give it a name and description, and select **Create repository**. Having done this, some instructions will appear on the screen that will help you to set up a connection between this remote repository and the local version on your machine. At the time of writing, the simplest way of doing this is the third box down. Keep these instructions as you will need them later, but for now, we need to configure RStudio a little further. Go to the **Tools | Global** options, and select the **Git/SVN** tab. The following menu will appear:

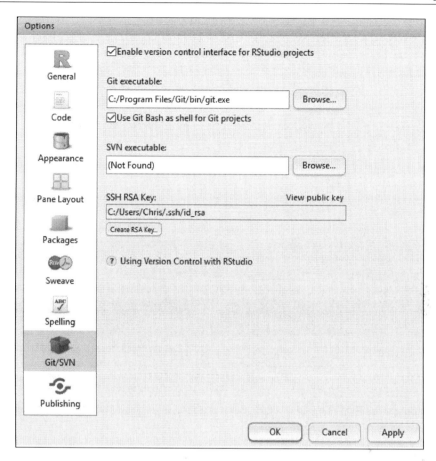

Check whether the Git executable is set up correctly in the first line. If you already have an SSH RSA key, then it should be displayed in the bottom line. If not, click on **Create RSA Key**, and you will be guided to create one. If you have not previously paired your RSA key with your GitHub account (which you would not have done if this was your first experience with GitHub), click on **View public key** above the third line, and then copy the resulting text into your GitHub account by going to your account settings. This can be achieved by clicking on your user portrait at the top-right corner of the GitHub web page. Next, click on **Settings**, and then click on the left-hand side of the screen and select **SSH keys**, and finally, click on **Add SSH key**, paste your key, and click on **Add key**.

Having done this, you will need to commit your code to Git, that is, to the local copy on your machine. This is very easy in RStudio. Select the **Git** tab in the environment pane in RStudio (by default, it's the top-right tab on the screen), as shown in the following screenshot:

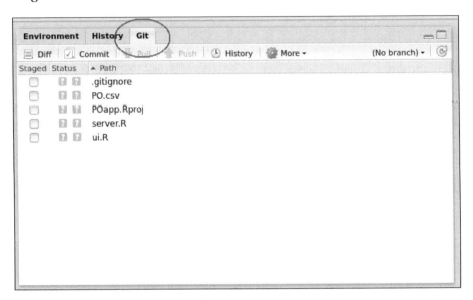

Select the elements that you want to commit by clicking on the boxes to the far left of the screenshot. This will be anything that you want to commit to Git for your first submission and anything that has changed for subsequent submissions. Click on **Commit** in the menu bar, which is visible in the screenshot. You will be prompted to review the changes in a new window as well as instructed to write a commit message in the top-right corner of this window. You cannot commit without a message. For your first commit, you might like to write `First commit of beta version`, and then for subsequent commits, you might make comments such as `Fixed jQuery bug`, `Added dashboard elements`, and so on, depending on the changes you have made.

Finally, to push to GitHub for the first time, select **More | Shell** in the **Git** tab. This will open a terminal window. Remember the terminal commands that the GitHub web page gave us when we set up the new repository and the two-liner I told you to keep track of? This is where we need this. Line by line, copy the two-liner from the web page. This will set up the connection between RStudio and GitHub. From now on, you can push your code (that is, upload it to GitHub) by committing and clicking on the **Push** button in the **Git** tab menu bar.

This is a very brief introduction to Git, GitHub, and RStudio and is designed to get you started. There is much more to learn about how to use these tools efficiently, and you are advised to take a look at the online documentation for all the three in order to learn how to make this process even simpler and more powerful.

Sharing applications using Git

We need to consult the websites mentioned earlier for more details of each of these steps. Once you've set your Git version control and paired with an online repository at GitHub, you can very easily share your creations with anyone running the R and Shiny package using the `runGitHub()` command, which takes the name of the repository and the username as mandatory arguments. For example, to run the Google Analytics application from *Chapter 2, Building Your First Application*, just run the following code:

```
runGitHub("GoogleAnalytics2ndEdition", "ChrisBeeley")
```

Code and data are both automatically downloaded and run. If you are using RStudio and want to launch your own external browser, as opposed to using the one that is built-in, you need to add `launch.browser = TRUE`.

If you don't want or need version control and don't need data to be included in the download, a simpler option is to use Gist, which is also hosted at GitHub at `gist.github.com`.

Using Gist is simply a matter of visiting the URL, setting up an account, pasting your code into it, and giving the `server.R` and `ui.R` files the correct filenames. You will then have a URL using which you can show your code to others. Running this code from the Shiny package is just a matter of using `runGist()` with the URL or even using the unique numeric identifier from the URL:

```
runGist("https://gist.github.com/ChrisBeeley/a2f1d88dfedcd2e1cb59")
runGist("a2f1d88dfedcd2e1cb59")
```

These are all valid methods used to run the minimal example from *Chapter 2, Building Your First Application*.

Sharing using .zip and .tar

Probably the next most frictionless method of distributing a Shiny application to R users is by hosting either a `.zip` or `.tar` file of your application either over the Web or FTP. You will need somewhere to host the file, and then users can run the application using `runUrl()`, as follows:

```
runUrl("http://www.myserver/shinyapps/myshinyapp.zip")
```

 Note that this URL is not real. You need to replace it with the address of your own file.

Of course, you can distribute a `.zip` file any way you like— your users need to only unzip and then use `runApp()` from within the directory just as you do when testing the application. You can e-mail the file and distribute it on a USB drive for any method that you choose. The disadvantages of this method are, firstly, your users have to unzip the file themselves (although this is unlikely to confuse many R users) and, secondly, any changes made to the application will also need to be distributed manually.

Sharing with the world

In most cases, any serious work that you do with Shiny will at some point need to be shared with a non R-user, whether it's a nontechnical colleague in your department or the whole of the Internet. In this case, a bit more of the legwork falls onto you, but you should still be pleasantly surprised about how simple the process is. There are two options here: set up your own server or get a paid account with RStudio to do it for you.

Shinyapps.io

Shinyapps.io is RStudio's paid hosting for Shiny applications. At the time of writing, there is a tiered pricing structure, depending on the number of applications you wish to deploy, whether you need the authentication of users, the number of hours your applications will run per month, and so on.

You can set up a free account that, at the time of writing, allows five applications and 25 hours of application runtime a month. This is welcome; however, it is only suitable for a very small-scale use; a single tweet of your application on the #rstats hashtag is likely to bring enough traffic to your site to use all of the 25 hours in a very short order. Indeed, I have been linked to many shinyapps.io applications, which indicate that the account has exceeded the allocated hours this month and, therefore, do not work.

> Be warned, therefore, if you want the world to see your application, you either need to get a paid account or run your own server (more on which is explained later). Using this service does, of course, entail copying your code and/or data to a third-party, so if this is a problem for you again, you will need to take a look at hosting yourself on a server.

If you are using RStudio, then it is very easy to get an application on shinyapps. Whenever you have a Shiny application (that is, a `server.R` or `ui.R` file) open, you will find a little **Publish** icon in the upper-right corner of the editor, as shown in the following screenshot:

```
File    Edit    Code    View    Plots    Session    Build    Debug    Tools    Help

  server.R ×      ui.R ×                                                      Run App

  1
  2    library(shiny) # load Shiny at the top of both scripts
  3
  4    shinyServer(function(input, output) { # define application in here
  5
  6       output$textDisplay <- renderText({ # mark function as reactive
  7          # and assign to output$textDisplay for passing to ui.R
  8
  9          paste0("You said '", input$comment,          # from the text
  10                "'. There are ", nchar(input$comment), # input control as
  11                " characters in this.")                # defined in ui.R
  12
  13      })
  14
  15   })

  2:1    (Top Level)                                                         R Script
```

You will be prompted to install various things, depending on your OS and the configuration of your R installation. On Linux, you will probably save yourself a bit of configuration if you install the development version of R (r-base-dev on Ubuntu, available through the R metapackage on Fedora, and for other distributions or operating systems, refer to the relevant documentation).

For all operating systems, you will be prompted to install various R packages. Users of Linux may have problems with configuring some of these packages; you may need to install libcurl-dev and openssl-dev (or their equivalent for your distro). In Windows, in my experience, the whole operation right from the vanilla installation of R is completely seamless and everything will be installed and configured correctly.

Then, you will be prompted to go to your shinyapps.io account and log in, where you can authenticate RStudio. You can now publish it straight from RStudio:

1. Just press the button highlighted in the preceding screenshot, select the files to be uploaded (for example, the code and data files), and click on **Publish**.

2. It will launch a browser for you, so you can see the application for yourself and copy the link that needs to be shared.

3. If you forget the link, just log in to shinyapps.io—the link is available from your list of applications in the menu.

Shinyapps.io without RStudio

It's not necessary to use RStudio in order to use shinyapps.io; it's just a bit easier. You need to follow these steps:

1. If you're happier in another IDE, then you just need to ensure that you have the latest version of devtools installed:

   ```
   install.packages('devtools')
   ```

2. Install shinyapps:

   ```
   install_github('rstudio/shinyapps')
   ```

3. Load shinyapps:

   ```
   library(shinyapps)
   ```

4. Log in to your shinyapps.io account, copy the authorize token command from the tokens menu (token marked with xs here), and run it in your R session (note that this only has to be done once on each computer):

   ```
   shinyapps::setAccountInfo(name='chrisbeeley',
   token='XXXXXXXXXXXXXXXXXXXXXXXXX',
   secret='XXXXXXXXXXXXXXXXXX')
   ```

5. Set your working directory to the folder that holds your application:

   ```
   setwd("~/myShinyApp")
   ```

6. Finally, deploy:

```
deployApp()
```

 More details are available on RStudio's pages at `shiny.rstudio.com/articles/shinyapps.html`.

Shiny Server

If you want to host the applications yourself, then Shiny Server is available for Linux. Again, there are paid and free options. Shiny Server is totally free and open source, which is a great credit to Rstudio.

The paid version has a number of benefits. The main ones being the provision of support and extra features, particularly authentication (LDAP/PAM/Google accounts and running over SSL to encrypt data to and from the server). It also allows you to use multiple R processes to serve one application, supports multiple versions of R on the same server, and provides an admin dashboard that helps server administrators to monitor server load, concurrent connections, and so on.

 Binaries are available for Ubuntu, Red Hat, CentOS, and SUSE Enterprise, and for other distributions, it is possible to build from the source. The free version is, in my experience, stable and well-featured. Installation details can be found at `rstudio.com/products/shiny/download-server/`.

Follow the instructions mentioned previously to install, and using the default configuration, you should be able to navigate to a test Shiny application by going to `chrisbeeley.net:3838/shiny/01_hello/` in a web browser (replace the domain with your own URL). In order for Shiny Server to work, you need to open the relevant port (in this case, the default configuration, 3838) on your firewall. By default, applications are run from files located within `/srv/shiny-server`. You can include directories within this folder in order to organize your applications.

The administrators' guide, which is linked to and from the download page, includes a lot of details of how to configure Shiny Server. You may wish to change the port through which Shiny Server communicates (again, opening this port on your firewall), change the location of application files, or add several locations to application files, or something else entirely. The complete details are available in the documentation.

Installation on Ubuntu is embarrassingly easy; even with my limited knowledge of running Linux servers, I had it up and running on my personal server in less than an hour. It's run quite happily ever since. Mileage with other distributions will vary, although judging from forum and blog posts, people have successfully run it on quite a variety of distributions.

Depending on what you are doing with your application, one thing to be careful of is directory ownership and permissions. For example, one of my applications produces PDF files for download. This requires making Shiny the owner of the directory within the application folder, which houses the temporary files that are produced for download and making the directory writable.

In a corporate environment, you may also find that the port Shiny uses is blocked by the firewall—changing to a different port is simply a matter of editing the configuration file as detailed on the Shiny Server web page given previously. If you are in a corporate environment running Windows, it's worth noting that the open version runs fine on an Ubuntu server virtualized on Windows, in my experience. I couldn't speak for the paid version, and I'm sure RStudio would be happy to advise you if were thinking about paying for a license.

Scoping, loading, and reusing data in Shiny applications

Although loading and reusing data in Shiny applications is covered in this chapter, because it is most likely that these features would be used in a shinyapps.io hosted application, in fact much of it also applies to locally run Shiny applications.

If you use shinyapps.io, it will expect your application to be portable, that is, to avoid dependence on writing permanent changes to the local filesystem. This is because the application might be moved to another server for load balancing purposes, rendering changes to the previous local filesystem inaccessible. You can write temporary files while a user is connected to the application (for example, if the user uploads their own data, this can be saved temporarily) but any changes made will be lost when the user exits.

Depending on the environment in which you are running and the task you are carrying out with your Shiny application, it is usually a good practice in most cases to make all Shiny applications portable. By making the application portable, you can not only seamlessly switch to shinyapps.io (even if it is just to share a beta version with colleagues using a free account) but it also means that the application is portable across other contexts as well; for example, if you distribute it via a `.zip` file, change your computer, or migrate the server on which you run Shiny Server.

It is important, therefore, to understand the scoping of data within Shiny applications as well as the means of getting data in and out both temporarily and permanently.

Temporary data input/output

There are three levels of scoping within the temporary, portable part of a Shiny application:

- The lowest level is data that is read-only within each individual instance of a Shiny application. This level is quite useful if a user wants a fresh copy of data each time they visit the application (if data needs to be even fresher than this, it can be placed in a reactive function; for more details on controlling reactivity, refer to *Chapter 4, Taking Control of Reactivity, Inputs, and Outputs*). Any data loaded after the `shinyServer()` function will be scoped like this. Note that this data is only available from the `server.R` file and not from the `ui.R` file, which is loaded first.

- The next level up is data that is available to all instances of the application (again, just within `server.R`). This can be useful if there is a very large dataset that needs to be loaded or that needs significant processing; this can then be done the first time the application spins up, so users do not have to wait for it. Any data loaded before the `shinyServer()` function will be scoped in this way.

- Lastly, it is possible to make data available to `ui.R` and `server.R` across all functions by loading it in a file called `global.R`. It isn't very often that you would want to do this; I never have, but you may find it useful if you wish to configure your UI using data but don't want or need the extra code and processing time a dynamic UI would necessitate (for more information on dynamic UI elements, refer to *Chapter 4, Taking Control of Reactivity, Inputs, and Outputs*).

Remember that it is very easy to get data in and out of Shiny sessions (that is, temporarily) using the `fileInput()` and `downloadHandler()` functions, as discussed in *Chapter 4, Taking Control of Reactivity, Inputs, and Outputs*.

Permanent data functions

There are a couple of ways to make more permanent changes to files in a Shiny application. If you are running Shiny Server yourself, then you can use the local filesystem on your server. Obviously, this means that your application is no longer portable, but for a final implementation, which you are happy to run on that server on a long term basis, this might be the right decision.

If you wish to maintain portability, you can use various remote/cloud-based services, such as Amazon or Dropbox. Applications running on shinyapps are restricted only to cloud-based services, since this maintains their portability. Within these parameters, you can use whatever type of data you find easiest or most useful: CSV, .RData, SQL, NoSQL, and so on. There are many R packages, which can help you connect to local and remote data systems, such as RMySQL (for MySQL), googleSheets (for Google Sheets), rdrop2 (for Dropbox), RAmazonS3 (for Amazon), and new ones are being added all the time.

So, pick the type and location of data storage that best suits your app. Remember the scoping rules described in the previous section, and you should be able to make things work just the way you want them, all with R code from right within your Shiny application.

Browser compatibility

The last thing that you will need to worry about when sharing your creations with the world is browser compatibility. On the whole, it's reasonable to assume that most home users are running Internet Explorer 10 (or 11) or another reasonably well-featured and up-to-date browser. However, corporate environments can be quite different and, even today, they are notorious for using old versions of Internet Explorer. Clearly, the best solution is to use an up-to-date browser in your organization, but if this is not possible, then it's worth knowing the following.

When you launch a browser locally from your R session; for example, when you are writing your application, or running someone else's application with the methods in the earlier part of this chapter, only Internet Explorer 10+ is supported. However, when running over Shiny Server, Explorer 8 and 9 are both supported. Older versions of Shiny (0.7 and below) did work on IE7 in my experience, although it was never officially supported.

Summary

In this chapter, we learned several methods used for sharing your Shiny applications with the world. This process is very easy indeed with fellow users of R, and a little harder with the whole Internet, but however you do it, I'm sure you'll agree that it was relatively painless and worth the effort. In this chapter, we discussed how to use Git and GitHub (and Gist) and how to use them to share your code and applications with other R users. We also looked at distributing Shiny applications manually or over FTP to R users using `.zip` and `.tar` files. We covered hosting solutions to share your application with the whole Internet, including shinyapps and Shiny Server. Lastly, we discussed compatibility issues that Shiny has with old versions of Internet Explorer, and when you do, and don't need to worry about them.

Index

K

knitr
URL 100
used, for downloading reports 100

L

line chart 13
lists 8

M

magrittr package
URL 120
Markdown
reference link 16
matrices 9
messages, between client and server
dropdownDepend.js 68-71
sending 65, 66
server.R file 67, 68
ui.R file 66, 67
minimal example, of Shiny application
about 27
server.R file 30, 31
ui.R file 27-29
minimal HTML interface
about 56
index.html 56-58
server.R file 59, 60

N

navigation bar
ui.R file 118, 119
using 118
notifications
creating 122-124
URL 122
NVD3
URL 139

O

objects 11
outputs, Google Analytics application
map of users, across world 44, 45
text summary 41
trend graph 42, 43

P

Pandoc
installation link 24
Patient Opinion
URL 50
plotting
data, preparing for 15, 16
pop-ups
adding, to output 110
adding, with shinyBS 107, 108
progress bars 88

R

R
about 1
data, loading 89, 90
installing 2
learning 5
reference link, for installing 2
rCharts
about 147-149
URL 139
R community
creations, sharing over GitHub 156
creations, sharing with 155
R console 2, 3
reactive functions
running, over time 92, 93
using 93
reactive objects
about 40, 41
using 93
reactive programming, Shiny
reference link 31

T

tabPanel elements
  naming 84
tags
  reference link 29
threejs
  about 151, 152
  URL 140
tooltips
  adding, with shinyBS 107, 108

U

UI
  icons, adding 106
  streamlining, by hiding elements 84
ui.R file 136-140
ui.R of minimal example 27-29

V

validateToken() function 81
variables 7
variable types 9, 10

W

web application development
  code download, URL 134
widgets
  types 33, 34
withProgress() function 88

Thank you for buying
Web Application Development with R using Shiny
Second Edition

About Packt Publishing

Packt, pronounced 'packed', published its first book, *Mastering phpMyAdmin for Effective MySQL Management*, in April 2004, and subsequently continued to specialize in publishing highly focused books on specific technologies and solutions.

Our books and publications share the experiences of your fellow IT professionals in adapting and customizing today's systems, applications, and frameworks. Our solution-based books give you the knowledge and power to customize the software and technologies you're using to get the job done. Packt books are more specific and less general than the IT books you have seen in the past. Our unique business model allows us to bring you more focused information, giving you more of what you need to know, and less of what you don't.

Packt is a modern yet unique publishing company that focuses on producing quality, cutting-edge books for communities of developers, administrators, and newbies alike. For more information, please visit our website at www.packtpub.com.

About Packt Open Source

In 2010, Packt launched two new brands, Packt Open Source and Packt Enterprise, in order to continue its focus on specialization. This book is part of the Packt Open Source brand, home to books published on software built around open source licenses, and offering information to anybody from advanced developers to budding web designers. The Open Source brand also runs Packt's Open Source Royalty Scheme, by which Packt gives a royalty to each open source project about whose software a book is sold.

Writing for Packt

We welcome all inquiries from people who are interested in authoring. Book proposals should be sent to author@packtpub.com. If your book idea is still at an early stage and you would like to discuss it first before writing a formal book proposal, then please contact us; one of our commissioning editors will get in touch with you.

We're not just looking for published authors; if you have strong technical skills but no writing experience, our experienced editors can help you develop a writing career, or simply get some additional reward for your expertise.

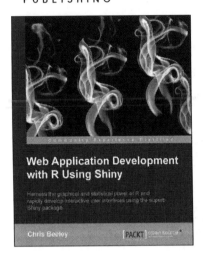

Web Application Development with R Using Shiny

ISBN: 978-1-78328-447-4   Paperback: 110 pages

Harness the graphical and statistical power of R and rapidly develop interactive user interfaces using the superb shiny package

1. Helps you to use Shiny's built in functions to produce engaging and useful user interfaces in hours, not days.

2. Enables you to extend Shiny using JavaScript and jQuery with minimal coding.

3. Shows you how to write cutting-edge interactive content for the Web.

Building Interactive Graphs with ggplot2 and Shiny [Video]

ISBN: 978-1-78328-433-7   Duration: 01:51 hours

Build stunning graphics and interactive visuals for real-time data analysis and visualization with ggplot2 and Shiny

1. Generate complex interactive web pages using R and produce publication-ready graphics in a principled manner.

2. Use aesthetics effectively to map your data into graphical elements.

3. Customize your graphs according to your specific needs without wasting time on programming issues.

Please check **www.PacktPub.com** for information on our titles

HTML5 and CSS3 Responsive
Web Design Cookbook

ISBN: 978-1-84969-544-2   Paperback: 204 pages

Learn the secrets of developing responsive websites
capable of interfacing with today's mobile Internet
devices

1. Learn the fundamental elements of writing
   responsive website code for all stages of the
   development lifecycle.

2. Create the ultimate code writer's resource using
   logical workflow layers.

3. Full of usable code for immediate use in your
   website projects.

Learning Data Mining with R

ISBN: 978-1-78398-210-3   Paperback: 314 pages

Develop key skills and techniques with R to create
and customize data mining algorithms

1. Develop a sound strategy for solving predictive
   modeling problems using the most popular
   data mining algorithms.

2. Gain understanding of the major methods of
   predictive modeling.

3. Packed with practical advice and tips to help
   you get to grips with data mining.

Please check **www.PacktPub.com** for information on our titles

66595380R00109

Made in the USA
Lexington, KY
20 August 2017